THE HUMANITY OF JEWISH LAW

THE
HUMANITY
OF JEWISH LAW

DAYAN DR. M.S. LEW
BA PhD

THE SONCINO PRESS   London — New York

First Edition 1985

ISBN 0-900689-87-0

Photo-typeset and printed in England by
G.J. George & Co Ltd.,
Topps House, St. Andrew's Mews
Dunsmure Road, London, N16 5HX

לזכר נשמת בננו היקר והבלתי־נשכח

הבחור **מתתיהו שמעון** נ״ע

TO THE CHERISHED MEMORY
OF OUR BELOVED SON

MERTON SIMON ע״ה

HE WAS ENDOWED WITH
DEEP FAITH AND HUMANITY.
HE RESTS IN THE HOLY LAND.

CONTENTS

ויגל כמים משפט וצדקה כנחל איתן

LET JUSTICE WELL UP AS WATERS
AND RIGHTEOUSNESS AS A MIGHTY STREAM

Amos 5,24

PREFACE

In this volume I hope to show that justice, equity and humanity are central to the Halachah, the Jewish legal system, and provide the key to its deeper understanding. I confess to an early interest in the subject. However, commitments as a member of the London Beth Din and Rabbi of the Hampstead Garden Suburb Synagogue delayed the writing and appearance of the book.

In preparing the work for publication I was fortunate in having the tender devotion and able assistance of my wife. Without her constant and caring collaboration I doubt if I could have accomplished my task. My gratitude to her is indeed deep and abiding.

The keen and active interest of our children, Gillian and Alan Feigenbaum and Estelle and John Lawrence, in the progress of the book has been a source of great encouragement. The diversions, varying in stimulus, of our grandchildren, Simone, Suzanne and Karen and Marc and Richard, were a joy amidst the demanding toil.

I should not omit to acknowledge the helpfulness of Mr. George M. Gee, J.P., past-President of the United Synagogue and Mr. Martin Clore who, together with members of my family and a group of personal kind friends, have advanced the publication of the book. To all of them I offer my warm thanks for their support and generosity.

I wish to take this opportunity to express my sincere appreciation of the sound advice and valuable suggestions I have had from Mrs. Phyllis Bloch, Director of the Soncino Press, Publishers.

My thanks are also due to G.J. George and Co. Ltd., the printers, for the meticulous care and attention they have given to the production of the volume.

If this book serves, with God's help, to afford a clearer insight into the concepts and moral values of the Halachah, the fount and inspiration of our great heritage, I shall feel amply rewarded.

London,
Shevat 5745
February 1985

INTRODUCTION

The purpose of this work is to show that the basic values and doctrines of Judaism are luminously revealed in Jewish law, known as the Halachah. Embedded in the vast Rabbinic literature, the Halachah is a rich repository of religion, law, ethics, traditions and customs. Its distinctive characteristic is the emphasis it places on strict compliance with the precepts of the Torah, the Divine Law, Written and Oral. The spirit that suffuses the Halachah and its teachings derives from religious roots, moral concepts and principles. Examples from Biblical and Rabbinic sources will serve to demonstrate deep humanity, justice and equity in a wide range of halachic rulings.

Yet it has been contended that Judaism based on the Halachah rests on an arid legalism with its sole concern for religious rites and observances, devoid of spiritual significance. The critics have clearly failed to discern the meaning and motivation of the ritual practices as well as the ideals and moral values that are central to the Halachah. Closer acquaintance with its teachings and postulates and with those who fashioned it may help to afford a fuller appreciation of its power and influence on the life and behaviour of the individual, the community and the Jewish people.

The Torah and the Talmud, the latter comprising the Mishnah and the Gemara, are the primary and fundamental sources of the Halachah. All subsequent codifications and commentaries rest essentially on these revealed sources.

The Sages, also known as the Rabbis, who shaped the Halachah were the spiritual descendants of the Prophets. Indeed, the ancient figures of the Fathers, Seers and Scribes stimulated their thought, fired their imagination and illumined their vision. Their over-riding concern was not with abstruse speculation but with man's conduct in life. Their aim was to teach the law, inspire and edify, and to instil in the people those virtues which would lead them in the path of justice and righteousness, peace and harmony, as defined and prescribed by the Halachah.

The Torah spoke in the language of man.[1] The Sages tried to follow the example. They often used terms current in their day. They were first and foremost erudite scholars, inspired teachers and eminent masters of the intellect. They had a remarkable gift of clear, concise and lucid exposition. But they were also men endowed with creative insights and poetic genius. Theirs was a rare and wonderful combination of profound perception and fervent spirituality.

Some Sages earned their living by manual labour. They were farmers or builders, artisans or tradesmen; some were physicians or followed other pursuits. Their *obiter dicta,* often expressed in aggadic language and incisive style, reflected halachic concepts and ideas as well as religious beliefs and doctrines, all revealing wisdom, vision and imagination. Some opened an halachic discourse with a Midrashic thought bearing on the

1. Berakoth 31b

subject under discussion. An arresting homiletical gleaning, they thought, would add interest, grace and elegance to the seriousness and solemnity of an eager and difficult halachic debate. The Sages believed that while the Aggadah was not granted the binding authority of the Halachah, it nevertheless formed an integral part of the Oral Law and they accorded it the same degree of holiness.

Their versatility was admirable and impressive. They had knowledge of scientific subjects as known in their time. Samuel, the famous Babylonian teacher, could justly claim "that the streets of the heavens (the courses of the stars) are as familiar to me as the streets of Nehardea".[2] They showed an understanding and sure sense of the characteristics of some foreign languages. Four languages ought to be employed, said a Rabbi of the third century: Greek for the art of song and poetry, Latin for appeal in military command, Aramaic was well-suited for elegies, and Hebrew, being clear and concise, for daily speech.[3] General and linguistic knowledge, they held, could be helpful in the interpretation and understanding of Jewish law.

But above all it was their piety and saintliness united with their august and dominant personalities that won them universal admiration, respect and reverence. And the esteem they commanded was of the purest quality and in full measure.

This fusion of outstanding qualities and towering talents gave them power and prestige, prominence and authority. Their words carried the same weight in questions of ritual and civil law as in wider national and

2. Ibid. 58b
3. J. Megillah 1,9

political issues. Their creative gifts drew strength and inspiration from their vigorous and vibrant minds and their warm and hospitable hearts. There is not a page in the vast and voluminous tractates of the Talmud which is not penetrated with their profound wisdom and nobility of spirit.

The Sages were known and admired for their candour and frankness, their simplicity and humility. These virtues they extolled and practised in their everyday life. It is related of R. Eleazar b. Harsom, a wealthy scholar of the second century, the owner of vast material possessions, that a bag of flour sufficed for his needs. He carried these spartan provisions on his back and travelled daily from teacher to teacher in order to pursue the study of the Torah.[4]

But the chief occupation of the Sages was with the interpretation of the Law which was the true and eternal revelation of God. Its teachings and doctrines were relevant to all times and circumstances. They were God's command. In simple but meaningful words they urged: "Study the Torah again and again, for everything is in it, and contemplate it and grow grey and old over it and turn not from it, for thou canst have no better rule than this."[5]

Concerned for the stability and continuity of the law, they gave sensitive and forceful expression to a significant dictum: "That the Torah may not be forgotten in Israel".[6] While this dictum generally applied to ritual observances and practices it reveals also their strong desire to preserve the power and vitality of the law in all situations.

---

4. Yoma 35b
5. Aboth 5,25
6. Temurah 14b

Embracing the whole domain of life, Jewish law paid due regard to the human condition with its difficulties and dilemmas. In the performance of the ritual observances the law demanded intention and devotion. In human relations it insisted on conscience and integrity, justice and truth. In a word, the Halachah demanded high standards of conduct in all aspects of life. Those who acted within the law but not in harmony with its spirit incurred the strong disapproval of the Sages.

In the chapters following it will be seen that the Halachah, far from being static and rigid, has been applied to changed conditions and situations. That justice and compassion motivated the many rabbinical and communal enactments and ordinances adopted and applied by the religious and lay leaders through the ages is further proof of a deep concern for the weal of the community, the welfare of the family and the rights and freedom of the individual.

A necessary warning must be added. Whilst in writing this book I have tried to make it of interest and value to the general reader and student, its material is not to be utilized to answer any halachic questions and difficulties that may be met. Such questions and uncertainties should be submitted to a competent rabbinical authority for decision in accordance with Jewish law and practice.

This book has been written in the firm conviction that the Halachah has been the life-giving force of Judaism and has helped, more than anything else, to preserve our great heritage. In a world faced with perplexing problems and predicaments and threatened with devastating dangers which obscure its vision, the message of the Halachah shows a road, sure and stable, leading to redemption, freedom and peace.

CHAPTER ONE

THE SANCTITY OF HUMAN LIFE

The sanctity of human life is a doctrine that pervades Jewish law. A Talmudic sage perceived this doctrine to be enshrined in the verse: "These are the generations of man in the day that God created man; in the likeness of God made He him".[1] The human personality is in the likeness of God and every human being has infinite value. Life is given to man in stewardship and he is in duty bound to preserve his life and health. Anything that is injurious to health is to be eschewed and is more zealously to be guarded against than even that which is ritually forbidden.[2]

The Biblical law, "an eye for an eye, a tooth for a tooth" is based on the concept of the dignity and worth of man and implies monetary indemnity. If in the course of a quarrel one inflicted an injury on a person, the Halachah states clearly the extent of the compensation to be paid. If the victim took to his bed but received no permanent injury he was to be paid for his enforced idleness, resultant loss of income and medical fees.[3] He was equally entitled to claim

1   Genesis 5,1; J. Nedarim 9,5
2   Ḥullin 10a חמירא סכנתא מאיסורא
3   Baba Kamma 91b

for the pain suffered and the humiliation sustained.[4] "Whoever humiliates his fellowman in public", the Talmud declares, "is as if he had shed blood,"[5] thus making the offence an act akin to murder.

Jewish law lays great stress on the dignity of every individual, both in life and death. For life in all its stages, from conception to the grave, is sacred. The fate of the unborn child and the life of the aged must be equally guarded. Life is a gift from God and it is imperative to view each person as uniquely valuable.

The Halachah distinguishes between an indignity suffered by an ordinary person or by a minor and that sustained by an important person.[6] If he is subjected to humiliation in public it is more serious than if he is insulted in privacy.[7]

The Biblical command "do not stand idly by the blood of your neighbour"[8] has been extended by the Sages to apply to a person who is able to save a life and does not. Thus if one sees another drowning in the sea or attacked by bandits or by a wild animal and refrains from rescuing him, he transgresses this precept. Briefly, danger enjoins rescue.[9] While the saving of one's own life takes precedence the security of the nation, according to one authority, manifestly comes first.[10]

The duty to rescue is variously defined in different systems

---

4   Exodus 21, 18-19; Maimonides: Ḥobel Umazik 2,11; Baba Kamma 85b cf. Tosafoth
5   Baba Metzia 58b
6   Tosefta Baba Kamma 9,12
7   Baba Kamma 86b
8   Leviticus 19,16
9   Sanhedrin 73a
10 Yeshuoth Yaakov, Responsa, Y.D. 157 holds that a person is permitted to sacrifice his own life in order to save a community or group. The author finds Talmudic support for his opinion in the incident of the martyrs of Lydda. From the latter he infers that one is permitted to sacrifice his life but there is no obligation on him to do so. Taanith 18b; Baba Bathra 10b

of law. The law in the United States of America has persistently refused to recognize, or at any rate, to enforce the
obligation of one person to come to the aid of another
human being who is in danger.[11]

The Mishnah rules that if Gentiles said to many women,
"Give us one from among you that we may defile her and if
not we will defile you all," let them defile them all but let
them not betray one soul from Israel.[12] No person may be
sacrificed to save others. However, if one particular woman
among them had been demanded she may be delivered up.
But if Gentiles wanted to kill a particular man of a group the
others may not deliver him up unless he had been legally
condemned to death. Some hold that if one man was singled
out it is permitted to deliver him up to save the rest.[13]

The story is told of Ulla bar Kushab who, sought by the
government, fled to Lydda and took shelter with
R. Joshua ben Levi. Troops surrounded the town and said
to the inhabitants, "If you will not surrender Ulla to us, we
shall destroy the town." Thereupon R. Joshua pleaded
with Kushab that he give himself up. He acquiesced.
Thenceforth, Elijah, who had been wont to reveal himself
to R. Joshua ceased to appear to him. After R. Joshua had
fasted many days, Elijah revealed himself again to him and
said "Shall I reveal myself to informers?" "Have I not
acted in accordance with the accepted code?" asked R.
Joshua. "But is that the code for saints?" retorted Elijah.[14]
This story is not so much to stress the standard required of
the saintly, but that in addition to the letter of the law there
is its moral aspect. The Halachah often draws attention to
a higher code to which all owe obedience.

11 Prof. Louis Waller, Rescue and the Common Law pp 141-157
12 Terumoth 8,12 cf. Tifereth Yisrael ad. loc
13 Maimonides: Yesode Hatorah 5,5; S.A.Y.D. 157, Rema 11
14 J. Terumoth 8,4

An incident recorded in the Bible[15] is a compelling example of a moral decision made by King David, a decision dictated by his conscience. We are told that David while engaged in war exploits against the Philistines had only a few of his best soldiers with him. A Philistine garrison was encamped in nearby Bethlehem where there was a well or cistern of water. David suffered from thirst and longed for a drink. The well, which he knew from his youth, was in the hands of the enemy and without any order from the King three of his men decided to break through the enemy's lines. With remarkable daring and total disregard for their own safety they reached the well, drew water and brought it back to the King. David's conscience, however, suddenly made him refuse to drink the water. Although most anxious to slake his thirst he felt he could not taste a sip. So determined, he poured the water on the ground as a drink offering, declaring solemnly, "Shall I drink the blood of men that went in danger of their lives?" The water having been obtained by his men in a spirit of self-sacrifice, David considered it too precious to satisfy his physical need. He treated the water as if it were consecrated to a higher purpose. The Bible does not record the moral principle that moved David. Perhaps it is too obvious to have needed elaboration. His action was clearly motivated by his conscience and moral feelings.

While the humanity underlying the rabbinic concept of saving of life overrides all religious commandments, yet the Halachah refers explicitly to the Sabbath laws which are fundamental to Judaism thus stressing the significance of פיקוח נפש. This finds sensitive expression in the Talmudic ruling that work permitted on the Sabbath for a dangerously sick person should preferably be done by a

15   II Samuel 23,15-17

Jew and not by a non-Jew.[16] The reason for this ruling? To demonstrate that the saving of life not only overrides the strict Sabbath laws[17] but must be performed as quickly as possible. Furthermore, it is rabbinically forbidden for a Jew who wishes to be religiously scrupulous to have the work performed by a non-Jew or a minor. This attitude might create the impression that the Rabbis, in permitting such work on the Sabbath, strained the law. It was also feared that should no non-Jew or minor be available, Jews would be reluctant to desecrate the Sabbath. This would cause delay and endanger life. The Rabbis were clearly exercised lest the sick receive not the speedy attention and treatment needed and which the Halachah expressly permitted. Isserls, known as the Rema, basing himself on an earlier authority,[18] held that if it were possible to have the treatment administered by a non-Jew without delay it was proper to do so. To reconcile this decision with the Talmudic ruling it has been suggested that what the Talmud implied was that it was not necessary to take steps to have the work carried out by a non-Jew but if one was readily available it should be done by him. The sentiment of piety, says Isserls, favours the latter view and is generally followed.[19]

The relaxation of the Sabbath restrictions in a public or national emergency further reflects the spirit which pervades Jewish law. "If Gentiles besieged a town in which there were Jewish inhabitants and the town is near the border that divides the land of Israel from the country of the invader, even if their intention is not to kill but concerns only material things, such as bricks and mortar,

16   Yoma 84b; Maimonides: Shabbath 2,3
17   S.A.O.H. 328,12
18   Ibid. Rema
19   Ibid. and Rav's Shulḥan Aruch ad loc.

the Jewish inhabitants are allowed to go out armed and to desecrate the Sabbath".[20] Isserls adds: "Even if they are on their way to besiege the town but have not yet reached it, the desecration of the Sabbath is permitted."[21]

The humanity which permeates the Halachah is reflected in the following Talmudic statement: "To save the life of an infant, even of one day old, we must desecrate the Sabbath but for David, King of Israel, when dead, we are not allowed to desecrate the Sabbath".[22] The Rabbis' concern for the life of the unborn child is touched with the same spirit. According to Maimonides the Talmudic Rabbis based their view on the principle that in emergencies of labour the unborn child is to be regarded as a "pursuer" threatening the life of the mother, and is in a sense to be considered as a malefactor towards her. The mother must, therefore, be protected against this danger even at the sacrifice of the unborn child. But if the greater part of the child was already born it may not be destroyed since the claim of one life cannot override the claim of another life. As can be seen from the words of the Talmud, if the mother dies while on the birth-stool everything is permitted to be done even on the Sabbath in order to deliver the child. While in all probability the child would have predeceased the mother, yet the possibility, however remote, of its survival renders the procedure

20 Erubin 45a; S.A.O.H. 329,6
21 S.A.O.H. 329,6: A discussion between the celebrated Harav Kook and a rabbinical correspondent is instructive. The latter contended that the law of פיקוח נפש only applied to an individual, arguing that belief in the indestructibility of the Jewish people is a basic doctrine of Judaism. Harav Kook replied that he was astounded to read the Rabbi's contention and he regarded his conclusion and attitude as bizarre. Harav Kook quoting an old source maintains that the concept of פיקוח נפש applies even more strictly when the safety and the life of the community, public or state is threatened.
    Responsa: Mishpat Kohen 144
22 Shabbath, 15b

mandatory. Isserls, however, following the view of the Gaonim, says that where the mother died whilst seated on the birth-stool, we are not permitted to desecrate the Sabbath in order to save the child. For the mother could be in a coma and the effort of saving the life of the child might shorten her life.[23]

In considering whether the principle of "saving of life" applies to a particular patient, it is essential to consult medical opinion. The Rabbis, we note, before they decided the law in medical cases sought the view of physicians.[24]

From a Talmudic ruling it is clear that the Sages were greatly concerned about the safety of the public.[25] According to Rashi and others greater leniency may be allowed in the case of a rabbinically ordained prohibition. Another opinion[26] holds that even in the case of a Biblical prohibition where there is a public danger a lenient view is permitted. The Ran took the ruling to mean that danger to the public comes under the rule of danger to life.[27]

Maimonides also refers to measures that must be taken on the Sabbath to prevent accidents and injuries to the public.[28] It is also permitted to extinguish a fire on the Sabbath even if it is remotely likely to endanger life.[29]

---

23 Oholoth 7,6; Arachin 7 a-b; Maimonides: Rotzeaḥ 1,6-8; S.A.O.H. 330, 5, Rema. In Jewish law, unless the life or health, physical or mental, of the mother is threatened, abortion is forbidden on the ground, inter alia, that it is tantamount to the destruction of potential life. See Chief Rabbi Isser Yehuda Unterman, Noam 6 p. 9; Dayan L. Grossnass, Responsa: Lev Aryeh Part 2, 32.

24 Nazir 52a

25 Shabbath 42a

26 Ibid. See Ran ad loc.

27 Ibid.

28 Shabbath 10,25; See also Maggid Mishneh ad loc.

29 S.A.O.H. 334,26 ff

A contemporary Halachist argues that the police may carry out their duties on the Sabbath in order to protect persons against danger and damage.[30]

The Halachah and medical science are at one in their concern for the saving of life and the protection of health. Maimonides ruled that only a child about which there is a certainty that it has no ailment may be circumcised on the eighth day. For peril to life overrides every other consideration, adding that while it is possible to postpone the circumcision a life lost cannot be restored.[31]

The Rabbis also paid due regard to mental health and well-being. In cases of rabbinic prohibitions they permitted patients afflicted with mental illness and those attendant on them to desecrate the Sabbath. They stated the grounds succinctly: that the patient's mind may not be further disturbed.[32] Concern for the mentally sick caused the Rabbis to take a lenient view in regard to the various modes of acquisition laid down in Jewish law.[33] In their condition the normal procedure might embarrass them.

We have seen that it is obligatory to disregard the Sabbath laws for the sake of one who is dangerously ill. If such a patient refuses to receive treatment because it would entail a violation of a Sabbath prohibition, he should be compelled to submit. For it is a grave sin for him to refuse to be cured.[34]

The Talmud relates the story of the last moments of one of its famous teachers. His students prayed for his recovery, which delayed his death, but his pious maid

30   Rabbi Shaul Israeli, Hatorah VeHamedinah vols 7-8 pp 335-347
31   Milah 1,18
32   Maimonides: Shabbath 2,1-7.
33   Gittin 59a; Maimonides: Mechirah 29,5; S.A.H.M. 235,21
34   S.A.O.H. 328,2; Mishnah Berurah ad loc. 6

interrupted their intercession pleading with them that their prayers were only prolonging the Master's agony. The Talmud praises her action. This incident is a commentary on two different attitudes. While the students, in accordance with the Halachah, felt it proper to pray for the Master's life, the devoted attendant thought that it was not right for human beings to implore God to change his design and purpose and thus prolong the suffering of another.[35]

The ruling that nothing may be said or done that may make a patient aware of the seriousness of his condition reflects the humanity of the Halachah.[36] It is clear that even in the case of one whose chances of survival are minimal there remains the duty of prolonging his life as long as possible.[37]

An early Talmudic teacher, Ben Patura,clearly held this view.[38] Although we know little about his life and learning, the fact that he was in dispute with and ventured an opinion contrary to that of the celebrated R. Akiba testifies to his own scholarly status and prestige. The case may have been of a purely academic nature, but it is illuminating in that it illustrates divergent points of view in a certain human situation. The question posed is instructive: Two men are travelling in the desert and one has a bottle of water containing a quantity enough to enable one of them to reach a place of habitation thus saving his life, but if they share the water both will die. Ben Patura held that it was right that both should share the water and die rather than the one who had the pitcher should stand by and see his companion perish. The

35   Ketuboth 104a
36   S.A.Y.D. 335,8
37   Ibid. 339,1
38   Baba Metzia 62a and Sifra 8,3

Scriptural injunction "that thy brother may live with thee"[39] was cited as the basis of his view. R. Akiba disagreed with Ben Patura's opinion, interpreting the words 'with thee' as implying that your life takes precedence over that of your brother.[40]

It is safe to suggest that it was not only deep compassion that lay behind Ben Patura's ruling but it was the moral duty devolving upon the one whose pitcher of water it was to prolong the life of his comrade even if it would inevitably be only for a brief period.

The sacredness of the human personality confers upon every man besides the right of life, also other rights.

Human life being sacred, Jewish law forbids suicide. The Rabbis found Biblical support for this prohibition in the verse: "And surely the blood of your life will I require".[41] These words, they said, contained the command against self-destruction.[42] An old tradition has it that a scholar who sacrifices his life for the sake of the Torah is not to be cited as an authority on matters of law.[43]

But to avoid transgressing one of the three cardinal sins, idolatry, immorality — such as incest and adultery — and murder a person is permitted to surrender his life. The general ruling is: "Concerning every other law of the Torah, if a man is commanded 'Transgress and suffer not death' he may transgress and not suffer death, excepting the three cardinal sins mentioned."[44]

The Rabbis, however, showed a lenient attitude to

39   Leviticus 25,36
40   Sifra 8,3
41   Genesis 9,5
42   Rashi ad loc.
43   Baba Kamma 61a
44   Sanhedrin 74a

those who committed suicide. In cases of doubt as to whether the person was of sound mind when he committed the act, certain rigid rules were relaxed.[45] If a minor committed suicide it was considered that he was of unsound mind. The later authorities, too, showed a liberal attitude in this matter. They were lenient in the case of self-immolation by those who did so in order to avoid excessive pain and suffering.[46]

R. Meir b. Baruch of Rothenburg (d. 1293),[47] the greatest rabbinic figure of Franco-German Jewry of the 13th century, refers to the following tragic incident. In April 1265, twenty Jews were killed in the city of Koblenz. At that time a Jew put an end to the life of his wife and four children to save them from torture and conversion. He intended to kill himself, too, but was providentially saved before he could take his own life. R. Meir was asked whether the unfortunate man was obliged to do penance for the murder of his family. In R. Meir's opinion suicide is permitted if the aim is to avoid forcible conversion to another faith. He quotes an old source[48] which explicitly exempts certain cases from the sin of suicide. The case of King Saul is cited as an example. He fell upon his spear to bring about his death in order to avoid being tortured by the Philistines.[49] An ancient tradition says[50] that Saul did not act improperly. Afraid of torture and suffering he was permitted to seek a way to meet his death.[51] The Rabbis declared that King

---

45 Semaḥoth 2,2; Maimonides: Ebel 1,11; Tur Y.D. 345
46 Gittin 57b; S.A.Y.D. 345,3
47 Responsa, part 2,59
48 Ibid.
49 I Samuel 31,1-5; II Samuel 1,1-10
50 Genesis Rabbah 34,19
51 Ibid.

Saul deserved a proper eulogy as his action was not contrary to the law.[52]

In his Responsum, R. Meir refers to the Talmud[53] which approved the action of the young men and women who threw themselves into the sea. They had been captured and taken to Rome for immoral purposes and they decided to take their lives rather than submit, by force, to outrageous conduct. While this was a case of suicide, he wonders whether it could be equally permitted to end the lives of others in order to prevent their forcible conversion and to enable them to "sanctify God's name". He concludes that because the distressed man followed the example of the saints who did take their own lives and killed their families when threatened with forcible conversion, no penance on his part was necessary. Indeed, if this man were required to do penance it would cast doubt on the conduct of the saints of old.

Another Responsum of R. Meir provides a further example of his deep humanity.[54] He was asked whether a deformed man may act as a Reader in the Synagogue. He replied in the affirmative. Physical deformities, he says, are a disqualification only for priests who officiated in the Temple. Indeed, he argues that a physical defect in a Reader, far from being a disqualification, is a virtue. A human king uses whole vessels and rejects those that are broken. God prefers broken vessels, for in the words of the Psalmist[55] "a broken and contrite heart, O God, Thou wilt not despise".

While the duty of visiting the sick is included in the wider term of גמילות חסדים "acts of lovingkindness" it is

52 Yebamoth 78b; Rosh at end of Moed Katan
53 Gittin 57b
54 Responsa: Part I, 23
55 Psalm 51,19

also referred to explicitly. The Mishnah[56] gives a list of good deeds that bear fruit here on earth and earn bliss in the future life. Ten acts, say the Rabbis, promote human well-being and the man who performs any of these acts himself enjoys happiness in this life and can look forward to reward and joy in the world to come.[57] Maimonides and the Code[58] devote entire sections to the rules of visiting the sick.

Maimonides held that this duty was rabbinically ordained but as it is included in the Golden Rule it has Biblical status. A Mishnaic ruling declares that there is no limit to this duty.[59] If one makes a number of visits the same day, each one counts as a *mitzvah*. Isserls[60] ruled that the duty of visiting the sick was only properly fulfilled if the visitor offered a prayer for the patient. However, it was not obligatory to do so in his presence for it may frighten and distress him.

That the Halachah enjoins tact, delicacy and sympathy on the part of the visitor is evident from other rules related to visiting the sick. As a physician, Maimonides[61] advised not to visit during certain hours of the day as the patient may be receiving medical treatment. The visitor must pay attention to the needs of the patient. He must do nothing that may sadden or depress him.

We have seen that concern for the welfare and dignity of fellowmen pervades Jewish law. To aid a person who is suffering is not only a kind deed, a virtue, but also a human duty.

56   Peah 1,1; cf. A. Marmorstein, Studies in Jewish Theology, p. 115
57   Baba Metzia 30b
58   Ebel 14,1 and 5; S.A.Y.D. 335
59   Peah 1,1
60   S.A.Y.D. 335,4 Rema
61   Ebel 14,5

R. Akiba said that one who does not visit the sick
commits a grave sin, for by his neglect to uphold their
spirit, he contributes to the aggravation of the illness. The
Sages had a knowledge of human psychology and the way
a sick man reacts when he is paid kind and gentle
attention. The Rabbis knew that a visit by a good and
sincere friend may enhance the patient's power of
resistance and encourage him to fight for his life. Their
belief found expression in an interesting utterance:
"Anyone who visits a sick person takes away a sixtieth
part of his disease or ailment", meaning thereby, no
doubt, that the visit helps to contribute towards the
patient's resilience and ultimate recovery.[62] A medieval
moralist taught: "When two people are sick and one is
rich and the other poor, it is the duty to visit the poor one,
for many will visit the rich person but few will visit the
poor one".[63]

To comfort the bereaved is another human duty and
the laws of mourning seem to respond to the mood in
which the bereaved find themselves in the early days of
distress and grief. Respect for the departed, preoccupa-
tion with the duty of arranging for the burial and the
concentration which the performance of religious duties
such as *tefillin*, prayer etc. require, are clearly behind the
laws governing אנינות. Accordingly, mourners are
exempted from all positive commandments during the
onan period.[64] During *shivah* the mourner is not
permitted to work or pursue his mundane interests. This
period of time was to be set aside for grief, meditation and
spiritual improvement. The eminent Rabbi J.B.
Soloveitchik writes. "Mourning in Halachah consists of

---

62   Nedarim 40a
63   Sefer Hassidim 361
64   S.A.Y.D. 341,1

more than performance of external ritual or ceremony. It is far more than that. It is an inner experience of black despair, of complete existential failure, of the absurdity of being".[65] He sees in the laws of *shivah* a means for creating a mood conducive and leading to repentance. The *shivah* prohibitions, he says, are like the prohibitions of Yom Kippur as is evident from the requirement to avoid washing, wearing shoes, using cosmetics and abstaining from marital relations.

Repentance would help to assuage the asperities of grief and the feelings of guilt and remorse which often oppress the mourners. The deceased was perhaps neglected in life, not having received what the mourner now considers as the care which should have been shown. Reflection during the period of intensive mourning would help to sustain the bereaved in the days of sorrow and distress. Having regard to the mourner's state of mind the Halachah relaxed its regime. Here we have another affirmation of the humanity of the Halachah and its concern with the psychology of the bereaved, his mental state and personal problems.

To argue that the rituals surrounding mourning were intended to lessen the trauma of death and bereavement is to detract from the deeper religious and spiritual aspect of the institution. The rites and customs of mourning are expressive of the faith of the Jew in his God in this time of crisis. Through observance of these laws and customs the mourner finds the support which sustains him in the sorrow of loss and in the poignancy of parting.

Like visiting the sick, comforting the mourners is a service which can be beneficently extended both to the poor and prosperous alike. While there is no explicit

65   Tradition, Special Issue, Spring 1978

precept in the Bible enjoining this virtue, the Rabbis regarded it as a religious duty. Perhaps, because compassion and sympathy with the distressed and suffering was a Jewish characteristic there was no need to legislate for it. That comforting mourners was a universal practice in ancient Israel may be seen from the Book of Job.[66] "When Job's three friends heard of the evil that was come upon him they came everyone from his own place to 'bemoan him and to comfort him'." They came to comfort him at the death of his children and "Sat down with him on the ground seven days and seven nights and none spoke a word unto him; for they saw that his grief was very great".[67]

The Mishnah rules that one may not comfort the mourner before the burial[68] when his grief is at its most intense. "When one visits a house of mourning", a Sage said, "one receives reward not for speaking comforting words, but for remaining silent".[69]

The many statements in the Talmud, Midrashim and the Codes relating to the duty to comfort the mourners, testify to the universality of the practice. A Mishnaic statement is striking evidence of the concern and sympathy for the mourner.[70] All who entered the Temple Mount entered on the right side and on leaving turned to the left, but a mourner turned immediately to the left. He was asked, "Why do you enter on the left?" He answered, "Because I am a mourner". All the people around him called out, "God who dwelleth in this Temple shall comfort you". The community shared fully and publicly

66   Job 2, 11-13
67   Ibid.
68   Aboth 4,18
69   Berakoth 6b
70   Middoth 2,2

in the individual's mourning. In the course of history, custom changed. A Talmudic source[71] states that after the morning service on the Sabbath the mourners left the Synagogue, tarried for a time in the entrance where they recited a special mourner's benediction and the *Kaddish*. The congregation stood around in silence thus manifesting their participation in the mourner's grief. Since the Middle Ages the custom, in modified form, has continued in many synagogues. On the eve of the Sabbath during the week of mourning, before Psalm 92 is recited by the Reader and the congregation, the mourner enters the Synagogue from the vestibule where he is met by the religious head of the congregation with the words, "May the Omnipresent comfort you among the mourners of Zion and Jerusalem". That the Rabbis allowed the practice during the Friday Evening Service although there was no public mourning on the Sabbath testifies to their regard for the feelings and emotions of the bereaved.

The foregoing pages bear witness to the profound concern of the Halachah for the sanctity of the human kind. To destroy or shorten life is to lay hands, as it were, on the Divine image. Any action that causes loss of or shortening of life, regardless of its high motives and sentiments, is in conflict with Jewish law.[72]

It is related of the sainted Rabbi Ḥanina ben Teradion[73] that during the Roman persecution he was found teaching the law in spite of the Imperial decree and was condemned to be burned together with the Sacred Scroll. His students, sorrowing witnesses of his terrible

71 Soferim 19,12
72 S.A.Y.D. 339,1 cf. Rabbi I.J. Weiss, the illustrious Halachist and Ab Beth Din of the Edah Ḥaredith, Jerusalem, Responsa: Minḥath Yitzḥak vol. 5,7-8.
73 Abodah Zarah 18a

suffering, stood in awe wondering at the marvellous fortitude and resignation of the Master, who was smiling amidst his agonizing pain. "What seest thou, O Master, that causes thee to smile in this tragic moment?", they asked. "I see the parchments of the Scroll of the Law consumed to ashes, but the letters, as if written in fire, rise up to heaven", he replied. "Open then thy mouth", said the horror-stricken and despondent disciples, "so that the fire enter thee". He replied, solemnly and humbly, "Let Him who gave me my soul take it away, but no man should inflict injury upon himself".

It is clear that like his fellow martyr, R. Akiba, he longed for the moment when he could make the supreme sacrifice, even amidst the most poignant suffering, thus manifesting the love of God with his whole life. That the saintly teacher did not heed the appeal of his grief-stricken pupils to help himself put an end to his agony is evidence of his determination to desist from any action that would bring his life to a speedy close.

Euthanasia, voluntary or otherwise, is in Jewish law tantamount to homicide. Accordingly, legislation that would empower doctors to hasten the death of a patient suffering from a terminal disease would be contrary to Jewish teaching and the Jewish conscience.

As already mentioned, nothing may be done that will disturb a patient's mind and equilibrium. But what greater agony can be caused to the sick, both young and old, than to manifest utter despair of their condition. The sense of being forsaken is bound to fill them with apprehension, diminishing faith and hope. Besides, experience has shown that diagnosis may be mistaken and that an entirely unexpected recovery may take place. A malady considered incurable today may be curable with further scientific advances and painstaking research. Many doctors know and tell of patients who have survived conditions regarded as lethal by all medical canons. These may be remote possibilities but the sacredness of human life is a compelling reason for taking into account such occurrences. Happily, the old and sick cling to life with remarkable tenacity. They clasp it close because in addition to the physical vitality and mental faculties there is the spirit in man that acts persistently by its own will and impetus.

Indeed, the spirit with which man is endowed distinguishes him from all other beings. Will-power and the zest for life, according to Proverbs, can overcome physical weakness and enable a person to recover from serious illness. But when a patient's will-power is undermined he will succumb. "The spirit of man will sustain his infirmity, but a broken spirit who can endure?"[74]

The remarkable modern medical procedures, such as heart transplants, artificial insemination, in vitro fertilisation and surrogate motherhood are beset with complex halachic problems.

Contemporary Halachists have devoted painstaking research to many of these problems in scholarly Responsa and studies.[75] It is not within the scope of this work to attempt even the briefest summary of the learned contributions. But it must be said that the implications of the new developments in human fertilisation and embryology present a formidable challenge from many points of view, halachic, ethical and legal.

74 Proverbs 17,22
75 See Chief Rabbi Sir Immanuel Jakobovits, Jewish Medical Ethics, a comprehensive and authoritative work in which he cites the literature on this wide-ranging subject.

Indeed, in our sophisticated society the subject of medical ethics has been exercising the minds of doctors, legislators and religious leaders. There can be, it is generally agreed, no swift and facile judgment or determination. For, the new and remarkable knowledge, so wonderfully gained, bears the message of fresh hope and trust as well as its burden of doubt, danger and frustration. The many and alarming problems that emerge demand long and anxious thought and deliberation. Man created in the image of God is endowed with a mind, heart and soul. Reared in love, devotion and tenderness, he is possessed of feeling, humanity and compassion. Our high regard for life, life sacred, precious and blessed, imposes the duty to preserve it under all circumstances, regardless of material cost and human exertion. The mystery of life is vast and deep. It belongs to a realm which man with his finite mind cannot penetrate. In that realm the Creator of life and light alone has sovereignty.

CHAPTER TWO

LAW AND MORAL VALUES

Jewish law finds its full expression in the Torah, the Talmud, the Codes and the Responsa literature. In these sources the fundamental rights and duties of man are propounded with power, insight and illumination. The Biblical maxim, "righteousness exalteth a nation" reflects the highest concept of the moral law which must be the code of conduct, guide and inspiration of individuals and nations alike. Jewish teaching insists on self-discipline, honesty, truthfulness and respect for other persons' rights and property. The rules of conduct are comprehensively formulated in Jewish legislation. The many disasters and tragedies of the world have been due to a disregard of the moral law. "Let justice pierce the mountain" is the maxim attributed to Moses.[1]

Justice is the foundation of Jewish morality and in the application of the law all are equal. There must be one law for the poor and the prosperous. There must be neither prejudice nor sentiment. Insistence of the strictest impartiality is expressed, simply and forcefully, in the injunction: "Ye shall do no unrighteousness in judgment;

1 Sanhedrin 6b

thou shalt not respect the poor, nor favour the person of the mighty, but in righteousness shalt thou judge thy neighbour".[2] Again the Bible warns, "Thou shalt not favour a poor man in his cause".[3] To favour either man in judgment is to pervert justice. While to help the poor is enjoined as a duty, the judge must not give a biased verdict in favour of the poor. The importance of the fairness of the judge was stressed by the Sages.[4] "Do not say this party is poor and the other is rich and it is the latter's duty to support the poor, I will decide therefore in favour of the poor and he will thus be maintained graciously". Nor must the judge say, "This man is important and influential and how can I put him to shame by finding against him?" There is to be no prejudice in favour of the rich and powerful. The oppressed, the weak, the slave and the stranger found protection in Jewish law. Man's injustice to man provokes the anger of God.[5]

Indeed, the spirit of justice permeates Talmudic teaching. Justice, truth and peace are the three foundations upon which the world rests.[6] Where right is suppressed war comes to the world.[7]

Jewish law governs all aspects of life which must be dominated by moral principles and values. The good life must embrace ethics, equality, freedom and benevolence. Man's dignity, honour and self-respect dictate the acceptance by him of collective obligations and responsibilities towards his fellowmen regardless of status or class.

2   Leviticus 19,15
3   Exodus 23,3
4   Sifra on Leviticus 19, 37-38
5   Exodus 21,22; Deuteronomy 21,15-20; Isaiah 1,17
6   Aboth 1,18
7   Ibid. 4,8

It is generally accepted that law is dependent on external sanctions and while the courts can enforce the law they cannot enforce moral duties. For morality depends on the conscience of the individual. It demands a higher code of conduct and willingness to surrender rights and forfeit privileges in certain situations.

It is significant that neither the Torah nor the Prophets draw a distinction between law and morals. The Ten Commandments contain prohibitions such as "Thou shalt not murder" and "Thou shalt not steal" as well as moral precepts, e.g. "Thou shalt not covet". In Judaism law and morality are indissolubly linked. Legal enactments and rules of conduct stemmed from moral values and sentiments. The commandments were given to Israel to live by them.[8]

To seek redress for wrongs in law is a fundamental human right. In doing so a man does not only protect his own interests but also helps to establish personal rights. Surrender of his rights could cause damage to others in society. Indeed, justice gives power to the powerless, strength to the weak, encouragement and support to the deprived. Law is a necessity in society as we know it. But the Prophets' vision was of a time of love and kindness and compassion to all. They spoke of the brotherhood of man as a corollary of the fatherhood of God. "Have not we all one Father? Hath not one God created us? Why do we deal treacherously one man against his brother by profaning the covenant of our fathers?"[9]

The hallmark of the righteous man is purity of heart and not the fear of sanctions and punishment. The ideal is exemplified in the story of R. Joshua b. Levi. He once

8   Tosefta Shabbath 16 end, quoting Leviticus 18,5
9   Malachi 2,10

wanted to curse a heretic who annoyed him,[10] but rather pronounced upon him the words of the Psalmist, "God's mercies extend over all His creatures".[11]

The Hebrew prophets preached justice and exhorted men to pursue it as a positive value leading to peace, confidence and security.[12] Present day society stands in urgent need of the rule of justice, law and order. To oppose evil and injustice with the force of law is a human duty.

Violence and oppression are repugnant to Jewish teaching.[13] As long as the strong oppress the weak it is man's duty not only to condemn it but also to fight against it. The controversy between R. Eliezer and the Sages regarding the carrying of certain weapons on the Sabbath reflects the individual attitudes of the disputants.[14] The Sages considered all weapons a reproach and unnecessary. They quote in support of their view Isaiah[15] whose vision of the Messianic times was when all weapons will be turned into instruments of peace. R. Eliezer, however, was of the opinion that these weapons were a man's adornments. It is safe to suggest that he deemed punitive weapons a necessity in the conditions of life in his time. As adornments and as defensive arms they were allowed to be carried on the Sabbath.

The humanity of the Sages is enshrined in their interpretation of the Biblical injunction against putting a stumbling-block before the blind, who may fall over to their hurt. The Rabbis saw in this a wider meaning, a

10   Berakoth 7a; Abodah Zarah 4b
11   Psalm 145,9
12   Isaiah 32,17
13   Berakoth 10a
14   Shabbath 6,4
15   Isaiah 2,4

prohibition against giving wrong advice to the uninformed. In their view it was also a warning against misleading the young, inexperienced and morally weak.

They further applied the prohibition to those who violated it in other ways. They included those who tempted the Nazirite to break his oath not to drink wine; to those who sold lethal weapons to weak and dangerous persons. They admonished fathers not to administer corporal punishment to grown-up sons. The sons may forget their filial duty and, in passionate and fierce anger, commit an unpardonable offence against their parents. To all these classes the Sages applied the injunction: "Thou shalt not put a stumbling-block before the blind".[16]

The injunction against cursing the deaf, although they cannot hear, equally included the defamation of anyone's character who cannot, owing to his ignorance of the slander, vindicate his own case or cause.[17] These ethical values of Jewish law testify to high moral concepts. To respect all men was a categorical duty.

It has been finely said that "what is not forbidden is not necessarily permitted."[18] There are cases in the Halachah that could in theory be permitted but sensitive and higher standards demand a stricter observance.[19]

In the view of the Rabbis all law is derived from the principles of justice and morality. A Talmudic ruling reflects this conviction. The reference is to two ships on a river which are so situated that if both pass together they will sink, but if they sail one after the other both will pass.

16 Leviticus 19,14; Pesaḥim 22b;Sifra on Leviticus 19,14
17 Ibid.
18 Edmond Cahn, The Moral Decision, p.85
19 Baba Metzia 30a-b; Yebamoth 21a; Moed Katan 5,a

Similarly with two camels.[20] In this ruling we discern an example of law dictated by moral considerations. In the case of one camel being laden and the other not laden, there is good reason that the latter should give precedence to the former. The legal decision flows from a moral judgment. But if both are in the same circumstances the law does not permit us to favour one against the other. Yet, should we say that both ships must sink or the two camels should fall by the wayside? Should we apply the legal principle rigidly? In such cases as these the duty devolves upon the court to urge a compromise which, in the Talmudic sense, means a decision based on the law but not in strict accordance with the letter of the law. The court has the power to ask one of the parties to surrender a legal right in favour of an opponent.[21] Accordingly, one of the ships is compelled to give up its right and allow the other to pass. The compromise serves as the basis of the general rule that any ship on the right side has the right of way and may pass before the other.

In Judaism justice is regarded as one of the three pillars upon which the world rests. Yet, the Rabbis equally praised its related aspects of equity and compromise. An equitable settlement which satisfies both parties to a dispute, but neither completely, is indeed a higher kind of justice. Kindness and humanity being the life-giving source of both justice and equity they enhance the final judgment. Such justice is pursued in a just way which is implicit in the Biblical words "Justice, justice shalt thou pursue". The Jerusalem Talmud reflects this idea in a meaningful utterance. "Wherever there is strict truth there cannot be a peaceful judgment, wherever there is

20 Sanhedrin 32b
21 S.A.Ḥ.M. 272,14

peaceful judgment there cannot be strict truth".[22] It is the kind of justice which finds expression in accommodation and which ensures peace between litigants.

While the Rabbis, in harmony with Biblical teaching,[23] stressed the importance of strict and impartial justice, they did not fail to commend the virtue of mercy. Indeed, even in capital cases Rabbi Tarfon and Rabbi Akiba[24] said they would have found good reasons for not applying the law, but they met with opposition. Rabban Simeon b. Gamaliel contended that such leniency would mitigate the deterrence of the law.[25] The two views may be said to represent two distinct attitudes to capital punishment. Neither could be ignored.

The concept of justice insists that a person can only be the plaintiff if he is involved and affected.[26] The Halachah forbids to cover up for transgressors of the law as in doing so we may endanger the lives of others.[27]

The men of the Great Assembly believed that in order to protect the law and the principles underlying it, it was essential to surround it with defensive rules and restrictions. Hence their familiar maxim: "Make a fence round the law."[28] Such "fences" would serve as precautionary measures against violating the law. Maimonides says that "the fence round the law" refers to the ordinances, enactments and customs which the need of the times required in order to strengthen faith and to improve society.[29]

22 Deuteronomy 16,20; J. Sanhedrin 1,1; cf. Tosefta Sanhedrin 1,3
23 Exodus 23,1-9; Leviticus 19,11-16
24 Makkoth 7a
25 Ibid.
26 Ketuboth 81b
27 Leviticus 19,16; Sifra on Leviticus 19
28 Aboth 1,1
29 Mamrim 1,2. The concept of "fences" in English law has been well

Many of the Sabbath laws were surrounded with restrictions designed to sustain those very laws. The handling of working tools, for example, is forbidden on the Sabbath not because of a direct prohibition but rather as a defensive rule against infringement of the basic law.

The Mishnah lists other examples. One must not climb a tree on the Sabbath. Nor is one permitted to ride an animal. The sanctity of the Sabbath, a fundamental and vital institution of Judaism, demands that its laws were to be protected by "fences". The Prophets exhorted the people to observe the Sabbath.[30] Those who violated the Sabbath in public, and wittingly, were liable to capital punishment.[31] The Rabbis accorded the same weight to the "fence" as to the basic law.[32] But as a general principle they never imposed an ordinance upon the community unless the majority of its members were able to endure it.[33] It will have been seen from these examples that the "fence", like the גזרה, ordinance, was a rabbinical institution introduced as a preventive measure. It is salutary to reflect that like the hedge, סייג, of a garden, which also serves to protect it against intruders, becomes part of the verdant and fragrant garden, so the "fences round the law" have become part of the living law.

The Rabbis had profound insight into the heart of the law in upholding high ethical standards. An enactment based on the injunction to do "what is right and good in

---

illustrated by Lord Devlin: The Enforcement of Morals p.29. With reference to the Licensing Act 1953 S.126 he writes; "A child of thirteen could probably take delivery of a pint of bitter in a jug without injury to his moral health". The act, however, forbids the selling of alcohol to children.

30   Isaiah 46,2; Jeremiah 17,11
31   Exodus 31,14-15; Numbers 15,32-36
32   Ketuboth 84a
33   Baba Kamma 79b

the eyes of the Lord"[34] concerns the case of a bankrupt. If his property was sold by order of the court, the buyer of the property was obliged to return it to the bankrupt whenever he was in a position to buy it back again.[35]

The Talmudic ruling that gave the adjoining neighbour the option of the first refusal בר מצרא was similarly based on an ethical and moral principle enshrined in the same precept. It was considered an advantage to have all one's properties adjacent to each other and therefore just and fair that a neighbour should have the first right of purchase.[36] According to some early halachic authorities the ruling is in the nature of a positive commandment.

Many regulations were laid down by the Rabbis in order to promote and protect business. Thus, if a man made a purchase in the open market of goods which turned out to be stolen, the purchaser was entitled, on returning the goods to the rightful owner, to recover from him the money paid for the articles. The owner could claim the amount from the thief. This ordinance was thought essential as many would be disinclined to buy goods offered in the market lest they be stolen. The ruling was designed to assist business, commerce and trade to function smoothly.[37] It was included among the "ordinances of the market". A similar principle is recognized in English law in regard to market overt.[38]

The problem of the protection of the third party is dealt with in Jewish law. The Mishnah declares: "If a man identified any of his articles or books in another person's possession and there had been a report of a burglary in

34 Deuteronomy 6,18
35 Baba Metzia 108b
36 Ibid 108a; Rashi ad loc.; Maimonides: Shechenim 12,5
37 Baba Kamma 15a
38 See M. Jung: The Jewish Law of Theft p.91ff

the city that such articles had been stolen, the purchaser
while pleading purchase in the open market must swear
to the owner and take the price he had paid from him and
restore the articles or books. In the absence of such a
report, the original owner has not established his claim,
for it may be argued that he first sold them to another
person from whom the defendant bought them".[39]

In Talmudic legislation if the owner despaired of
recovering the articles he thereby declared the articles
ownerless and there was no obligation on the part of the
purchaser to return them. But post-Talmudic authorities
ruled that even if the owner had abandoned hope of
recovering the articles, or if they had been transferred to
another domain, there was the obligation to return them
to the owner.[40]

The ruling that the owner could demand the return of
his stolen goods affected free commerce and trade.
Prospective purchasers were reluctant to buy anything
lest the owner come and prove his ownership. The purchaser would then lose the articles and the money he had
paid for them. According to the Mishnah the purchaser
was entitled to ask the owner to pay him the amount he
had paid for the articles before he restored them. This
ruling was based on the "ordinance of the market" תקנת
השוק. The purpose of the ordinance was to enable
business to proceed normally.[41] Maimonides explains the
underlying principle: "To buy from a thief the articles
that he had stolen is indeed sinful for it encourages
transgressors to steal more". If the thief will not find a
buyer he will refrain from stealing. Concerning receivers
Maimonides writes: "Whoso is a partner with a thief

39   Baba Kamma 114b
40   S.A.Ḥ.M. 356 cf. Rema; cf. M. Elon, Hamishpat Haivri vol.2 p.480 ff
41   Baba Kamma 115a

hateth his own soul".[42] The Talmudic dictum is apt. "It is not the mouse that is the real thief, but the hole where it hides that which it had taken".[43]

It is evident from the rulings and ordinances discussed that along with the concept of justice, which is central to Judaism, the ideals of equity and uprightness pervade the Halachah. For the Sages the words of the Torah "And thou shalt do that which is right and good in the eyes of the Lord"[44] implied that it is not enough to do that which is right, to act according to the strict letter of the law. For such action often involves hardship. The truly just must avoid taking advantage of strict legality. Indeed, while justice bids man do that which is right and keep faith, equity demands a greater justice, justice of a higher kind. It is perhaps this sense of justice that the phrase לפנים משורת הדין denotes. Accordingly, it ought to be rendered "within the line of justice". Justice demands adherence not merely to the letter of the law, but to that kind of justice which includes equity and uprightness. The Hebrew word לפנים bears this connotation.

The Talmud records the following case. A renowned scholar hired porters who negligently broke a barrel of wine. The men having failed to exercise due care, the scholar seized their cloaks as compensation for his loss. The aggrieved porters summoned him before the celebrated Rab, who ordered that the garments be returned. The scholar questioned Rab's decision. "Is this according to the law?", he asked. Rab said, "Yes, for it is written 'That thou mayest walk in the way of good men'".[45] The scholar obeyed the decision. The porters

42   Genevah 5,1; Proverbs 29,24
43   Gittin 45a לאו עכברא גנב אלא חורא גנב
44   Deuteronomy 6,18
45   Poverbs 2,20 and Baba Metzia 83a

thereupon appealed. They were poor men, they had
toiled a full day, they were fatigued and now they had
nothing for their labour. Rab ruled that their wages were
to be paid. The scholar again wondered if Rab's decision
was according to the *din*. Rab replied that his ruling was
according to the law, and quoted in support the
continuation of the verse mentioned earlier, "and keep
the paths of the righteous".[46]

The case is significant as a striking illustration of the
concept of justice and equity perceived by the Halachah.
When Rab declared that his decisions were in accordance
with the law, he thereby emphasized that the law was not
an end in itself, and that it was a moral obligation to act
beyond the strict letter of the law. He held that the law
was not something separate and apart from justice and
equity.

The high concept of equity as an integral part of the law
makes the Jewish legal system unique in character.
Accordingly, the courts applied both law and equity in
their jurisdiction and enforcement of the law. This
unified power had many advantages. It helped the courts
to mete out justice in the fullest sense of the term. By
harmonizing what was the strict law with the spirit of the
law they achieved what "is right and good in the eyes of
the Lord". It is in dispensing this kind of justice that the
Sages described the judge as being a partner with God.

The following two examples further reflect the unity of
law and equity in the Halachah.[47] "If one of the brothers
or partners sold his share to a stranger the other
brothers or partners had the right to pay out the buyer
and to take the property for themselves". Likewise, "if a

46   Ibid.
47   S.A.Ḥ.M. 175,5-6

man sells his property to another person, whether the owner himself sold it or his agent or the court, the nearest neighbour bordering on the property has the right to pay out the money to the buyer and acquire the property". The buyer would be regarded in point of law as having acquired the property, yet in equitable thinking the brothers or partners, or the neighbour who owns the property adjacent to the one sold, have a right to special consideration. Neighbourliness created human relations which imposed certain duties and obligations as well as rights and privileges. A Talmudic maxim gives the court the right to restrain a person from acting unfairly towards his neighbour. Such conduct is characterized as "the attribute of the people of Sodom" מידת סדום.

The concept of equity is implicit also in the following cases recorded in the Talmud. It is related of R. Ishmael b. Jose that he once met a man carrying logs of wood and he felt impelled to help him carry the burden. In law his age and status exempted him from this duty. R. Ishmael, however, acted in accordance with the principle of greater justice, "within the line of justice". Indeed, he regarded it his duty to help the man who was carrying the load.[48]

Another Talmudic teacher, R. Hiyyah, who was considered an expert on coins, was asked by a woman who kept a shop whether a certain coin was genuine. He told her that it was. She returned later and told him that she had ascertained that it was forged. He asked a colleague to change the coin for her and at the same time requested him to record that he, R. Hiyyah, had made a mistake. While the law did not oblige money changers to pay compensation for a mistake made by them, R. Hiyyah felt

48 Baba Metzia 30b

it his duty to comply with the demand implicit in the idea "within the line of justice".[49] Other scholars, too, we read, acted in accordance with the spirit of the principle of "within the line of justice".[50]

While the cases cited involved pious scholars who, doubtless, were imbued with higher standards of ethics, the principle would equally be applied by the court to others. That scholars were motivated by higher moral standards may be seen from the action of R. Pappa. He bought a field from a man who was in financial difficulties. When the man's position improved the scholar returned his field to him.[51] It is evident that in early Jewish law the idea of לפנים משורת הדין though based on a moral obligation, was part of the law and would be enforced.[52]

Rabban Simeon b. Gamaliel said "Society is preserved by truth, by justice and by peace."[53] Without these foundations the world could not exist. The Aggadah echoed a similar sentiment in a remarkable parable. It may be compared to a king who had empty drinking glasses. He said, "If I fill them with boiling water they will split, and if with cold they will contract". He mixed the hot with cold and the glasses remained sound.[54] So God created the world with His attributes of both justice and mercy which combine to help protect society from disintegration. Compassion divorced from law could generate violence.

There is a touch of superb sensitivity in the tradition in

49   Baba Kamma 99b
50   J. Baba Metzia 2,6
51   Baba Metzia 97a
52   Ketuboth 49b and Rashi ad loc.
53   Aboth 1,18
54   Genesis Rabbah, 12,15

which God is offering up a prayer that he may deal with His children "within the line of justice".[55] Rab said: the rule is that a man's lost property takes precedence over that of others, but one should act "within the line of justice", which he considered as binding upon the individual as the law.[56] We are told that R. Jonathan compelled sons to provide for their father's maintenance regardless of the strict law.[57]

It is informative that the Jewish legal system recognizes a concept of law which advocates a high moral standard expressed in the maxim of לפנים משורת הדין "within the line of justice". Because the Hebrew word חסיד in the Talmudic definition denotes a person who acts in conformity with the principle of מידת חסידות, the "attribute of piety", has been equated with the concept of "within the line of justice".[58] Maimonides is cited in support of this identification.[59] The Tosafoth Yomtov is also quoted as sharing this view.[60]

The Rabbis considered the law relating to certain voidable contracts. In such cases the plaintiff can only nurture a grievance or resentment תרעומת against the defendant or opponent.[61] But a man of character and righteousness would do his utmost to practise the "attribute of piety" in order to remove the cause of grievance against him.[62] This high notion of moral obligation is inherent in Jewish law.[63]

55 Berakoth 7a
56 Ibid.; S.A.H.M. 264,1
57 Ketuboth 49b
58 Baba Metzia 30b
59 Deoth 1,1
60 M. Sotah 9,15
61 Baba Metzia 75b ff
62 Ibid 52b
63 Ḥullin 130b

R. Joḥanan attributed the destruction of Jerusalem to the people of his generation who in their political and social relations insisted on the letter of the law and failed to show consideration for others.[64] In time of national danger the individual was to forfeit his own right and consider the needs of the community. The disregard of rabbinical law was also believed to be a reason for the national disaster.[65]

Those who surrendered their legal rights were commended for their action. Job, who forfeited his personal rights, was quoted as an example.[66] As already mentioned some post-Talmudic authorities ruled that the court could enforce a decision based on the principle of לפנים משורת הדין.[67]

The Bible postulates ethics, social and commercial, among its basic teachings.[68] Amos[69] condemned those who waited for an opportunity to raise prices. Proverbs denounces those who inflate prices especially in a time of scarcity. "He that withholdeth corn, the people shall curse him".[70] The Talmud, likewise, disapproves of the practice. While the raising of prices of the necessities of life was against moral law it later formed part of Jewish legislation,[71] and the courts acted accordingly.[72] Maimonides ruled that punishment was to be meted out to those who raised prices. The community was duty bound to regulate commodity prices.

---

64   Baba Metzia 30b
65   Ibid. 88a
66   Job 1,1; Baba Bathra 15b; Megillah 28a
67   Baḥ on Tur Ḥ.M. 12,4
68   Leviticus 25, 14-17
69   Amos 8,4-6
70   Proverbs 11,26
71   Baba Bathra 90b
72   Ibid 89a; Mechirah 14,6; S.A.Ḥ.M. 231,25

Jewish law equally forbids overcharging and the amount overcharged was a determining factor. Rabba ruled that in the case of an overcharge of less than a sixth of the price, the sale is valid and the amount overcharged need not be returned. If the overcharge is exactly a sixth it must be returned but the sale is valid. An overcharge of more than a sixth invalidates the sale.[73]

According to the Mishnah[74] the law against defrauding applies to both the buyer and the seller. Just as the seller must not overcharge, the buyer must not pay less than the value of the goods bought. The laws against defrauding apply to chattels only. Real estate is not subject to the same regulations.[75] Indeed, some authorities would limit the overcharge to less than half of the actual value in the case of immovable property.[76]

The concept of charity in Jewish teaching is wide-ranging. It includes the duty of lending to those in need.Charity must be practised for its own sake. The borrower must not reward the lender. Even an expression of gratitude and appreciation would detract from the benevolent deed. Lending must be motivated by humanity and sympathy. The Biblical prohibition of interest made money-lending a non-profitable activity. Consequently lenders were unlikely to advance money with the risks attached to business transactions without the compensation of interest. There was clearly a need for measures that would safeguard the interest of creditors. Alive to the commercial needs of the people, needs often aggravated by political and economic conditions, the Rabbis evolved a legal instrument, known as עיסקא,

73 Baba Metzia 49b; S.A.Ḥ.M. 227
74 Baba Metzia 4,4
75 Ibid. 4,9
76 Ibid.

literally business, occupation. Briefly, every sum
involved in a loan, especially when advanced for trading
purposes, was considered half as a loan and half as a trust
on which the lender was entitled to the larger share of the
profits.[77] This legal instrument was introduced to meet
the needs, within the framework of the Halachah, of an
urban society with its commerce and industry. It was
also, no doubt, to enable those in a position to practise
this form of economic aid. To avoid the prohibition of
usury the investor takes a greater share of the risk than of
the profit; he receives, for example, either half of the
profit but bears two thirds of the loss or a third of the
profit but bearing half of the loss. This arrangement was
considered by the Rabbis to meet the problems both of
the debtor and the creditor.

From the earliest times the law of interest had applied
to ordinary business transactions, and all benefits, in
whatever form, in return for the lending of money or for
the giving of credit were considered usurious. The Rabbis
condemned in scathing terms those who made a living by
usury. They disqualified them from acting as witnesses in
a court of law.[78]

A number of other adjustments in the existing law in
favour of creditors was necessary. Thus it was enacted
that creditors in collecting their debts from landed
property could insist on being paid out of the medium
quality despite the implied Biblical law that entitled the
debtor to discharge his liability by offering the creditor
inferior quality.[79]

While witnesses in all other monetary cases were

---

77   Baba Metzia 104b
78   Sanhedrin 24b; Maimonides: Eduth 10,4
79   Gittin 49b

subjected by the court to a searching cross-examination and scrutiny, in cases of indebtedness they were spared this ordeal.[80] It was further ordained that laymen were competent to try such cases, as against other monetary cases, which required for their adjudication a qualified judge.[81]

All these innovations were motivated by two considerations. Their purpose was to facilitate creditors in the recovery of their debts, so that, in the words of the Talmud, "prospective borrowers should not find the doors of the lender closed to them".[82] This fear caused the Rabbis to sanction departure from the old law. The changes were deemed necessary in order to encourage creditors to perform their religious and human duty. It was no doubt the same considerations that were responsible for the institution of the פרוזבול. Hillel had felt impelled to introduce this legal instrument in order to save debts from the operation of the laws of *shemittah,* the year of release.

The *prozbul* serves both as an illustration of the notion of the legal device and as an example of creative Halachah.[83] The institution was based on the text "that which is thine with thy brother, thine hand shall release".[84] Implicit in the Biblical text was the law that the year of release only affects debts of which the bonds remained in the possession of the lender. But if these had been delivered to the Beth Din before the intervention of the year of release, such debts being deemed virtually exacted, the prohibition "he shall not exact"[85] did not

80 Sanhedrin 3a
81 Ibid. 2b-3a
82 Ibid. 3a
83 Deuteronomy 15,1-3
84 Ibid.
85 Ibid.

apply. An extension of this precedent enabled Hillel to institute the *prozbul*.[86] It amounted to entrusting the court with the collection of the debt. Thus without actually handing over the bond to the Beth Din the creditor could secure the debt against forfeiture.[87]

· The institution of the *prozbul* was keenly debated by the Rabbis of the Talmud. They considered its validity and suggested various explanations.[88] Some scholars maintain that the aim of the *prozbul* was to establish, in changed circumstances, public credit on a safe basis and to facilitate business activities. A closer examination of Hillel's daring device, debated at length in the Talmud, will reveal that it was not only economic and social conditions but also moral and human considerations that were Hillel's motivation.

The Biblical command enjoining the Israelite not to harden his heart but to lend money to his neighbour in need[89] was at the very basis of the *prozbul*. Hillel feared that people would be unwilling to act according to the precept of the Torah.[90] He was concerned alike about the financial needs of the debtor as well as the moral well-being of the creditor. The operation of the *shemittah* year had the effect that people ceased lending each other money and thus transgressed the Biblical injunction. It is safe to suggest that Hillel recognised the necessity of a measure, within the framework of the law, that would prove of advantage to both creditor and debtor.

"Beware that there be not a base thought in thy heart,

---

86   Gittin 36a and Sifre Deuteronomy 15 ad loc.
87   Gittin 36a
88   Ibid 36a-b
89   Deuteronomy 15,7-9
90   Gittin 36a

saying, the seventh year, the year of release, is at hand".[91]
Indeed, the *prozbul,* Hillel believed, would be the means
of preventing the Torah precept which enjoined lending
money to the needy brother, from falling into disuse.
Hillel's justification was, therefore, the maintenance of
the Biblical command, which the operation of the law of
release threatened.

This suggested reason for the humanity implicit in the
legal justification for the *prozbul* finds support in the
following Talmudic passage.[92] "When R. Dimi came
(from Palestine to Babylon) he said 'Whence do we know
that if one is his neighbour's creditor for a מנה and knows
that he has not money (for payment) he may not even
pass in front of him? From the verse 'Thou shalt not be to
him as a creditor".[93] Indeed, the creditor was enjoined to
refrain from doing anything that may embarrass the man
who is indebted to him lest he feels ashamed. There can
hardly be a more sensitive attitude to a debtor whose
plight prevents him from meeting his obligation.

It was clearly a religious and moral as well as an
economic consideration that had prompted Hillel to
institute what was regarded by some of his successors, as
a radical innovation. But he, as already mentioned, was
profoundly concerned to preserve the Biblical law. By
means of the *prozbul,* the very principle underlying the
law was safeguarded in changed conditions of life.

91   Deuteronomy 15,9
92   Baba Metzia 75b: מנה a weight in gold or silver equal to one hundred
shekalim.
93   Exodus 22,24 and Rashi ad loc.

CHAPTER THREE

THE WORK OF JUSTICE

The institution of the Jewish courts of law goes back to the earliest Bible times. The Torah tells how Moses, after descending from Mount Sinai with the Tablets of the Law, sat alone, administering justice from morning to evening.[1] With Divine approval he appointed judges to try civil disputes. More serious cases and matters in doubt were still to be submitted to him for decision.

The early judges were known as rulers over groups of ten, fifty, one hundred and a thousand families.[2] Later the elders sitting in the city gateway functioned as judicial officers and were subject to the jurisdiction of the judges.[3]

The Talmud[4] casts light on the origin and development of the courts. The Codes equally devote detailed attention to the composition and procedures of the courts.[5] The regime of law is the foundation of Judaism.

The Sages discuss and analyse the history and respective functions of the various courts.[6] They define

[1] Exodus 18, 13
[2] Ibid.
[3] Tur H.M. beginning
[4] M. Sanhedrin 1,1; Sanhedrin 18b
[5] Tur H.M. beginning
[6] Sanhedrin 18b

the division of the courts. Monetary cases, they declare, required three judges to adjudicate. Maimonides[7] held that according to Biblical law one judge could sit in monetary cases relating to borrowing and lending but for robbery and assault three experts had to try such cases. To adjudicate criminal cases carrying corporal or capital punishment, courts consisting of twenty three members were essential.

The highest court, known as the Great Sanhedrin, consisted of 70 or 71 members. Scholars are not agreed as to the functions, powers and prestige of this historic, august and authoritative body. Indeed, some hold that the Great Sanhedrin comprised two bodies, one religious and one political. However, the Sanhedrin had jurisdiction in communal and national matters, clarified points of law in doubt, and pronounced on conflicting legal opinions. The Sanhedrin had also judicial oversight over the lower courts and functioned as a Supreme Court and as a legislature.

According to the Mishnah cases of borrowing and lending, like the cases of assault and robbery, had to be tried by three expert judges. The Rabbis, however, having regard to the needs of the times, ruled that in the former cases even three laymen could form a court. The reason given is that would-be creditors should not refuse to lend money[8] and the requirement of three competent judges in the event of a dispute might discourage lending.

It is significant that throughout the history of the Diaspora with its political, social and economic changes, the Jewish courts continued to function and to exercise full authority. The communal leaders pleaded and

7 Sanhedrin 5,8
8 Sanhedrin 2b-3a שלא תנעול דלת בפני לווין

pressed for their own courts in which the people had complete confidence and for which they entertained profound respect. Indeed, they regarded their courts as both religious and judicial institutions charged with the task of administering a law, inspired and informed by the Divine wisdom. Few failed to honour the summons and to obey strictly the decisions of the courts.

The judges were considered the guardians of the law and morality. They had to be possessed of many qualities and virtues. They were to be able men, God-fearing, men of truth, hating unjust gain.[9] They were to be men of unimpeachable character, piety and humanity.

In his wonderful picture of the future, Isaiah[10] ascribes to the ideal judge the following qualities. He must be wise, understanding and God-fearing. He must judge the poor and oppressed. To the Prophet's portrayal, the Talmud adds:[11] "Well versed in the battle of the Torah; able to deduce one thing from another; sustaining his ruling by weighty reasons". The judge, says Maimonides, must be so generously and spiritually endowed as not to cause damage to others.[12]

In Talmudic times many distinguished scholars shirked the office of judge because of its great responsibilities. There were those who were styled יראי הוראה "afraid to give decisions". Concerning that class R. Ishmael taught[13] "He who shuns judicial office (but seeks a friendly settlement) rids himself of hatred, robbery and perjury." As a judge he was known for his

---

9 Exodus 18,21 and Sanhedrin 93b
10 Isaiah 11,2-5
11 Sanhedrin 93b
12 Introduction to Seder Zeraim
13 Aboth 4,9

absolute integrity and saintly character.[14] His father, R. Jose ben Halafta, was admired for his great learning and modesty. "Follow Jose to Sepphoris" was advice given by the Sages to would-be litigants.[15]

The Hebrew Prophets rebuked those who perverted justice. "They have spoken words, swearing falsely in making a covenant; thus judgment springeth up as hemlock in the furrows of the field".[16] Amos likewise condemned those who practised injustice. "Ye who turn judgment to wormwood and cast off righteousness to the ground".[17] "For ye have turned judgment into gall, and the fruit of righteousness into hemlock".[18] These words were a challenge and a grave warning to legislator and judge alike.

The Rabbis of the Talmud required the judge to perceive the intention of the law as well as the claims of morality and humanity. If he is adjudicating in a case in which he suspects conspiracy[19] he is to heed the injunction of the Torah, "Keep thee far from a false matter".[20]

The words of the Torah, "Justice, justice shalt thou follow that thou mayest live and inherit the land which the Lord thy God giveth thee",[21] is taken to be addressed to a judge to act in accordance with the dictates of humanity.[22] Indeed, the Talmudic Sages speak critically

14 Makkoth 24a; Abodah Zarah 19b
15 Sanhedrin 32b
16 Hosea 1,4
17 Amos 5,7
18 Ibid. 6,12
19 Sanhedrin 32b
20 Exodus 23,7; Sanhedrin 32b, Tosafoth
21 Deuteronomy 16,20
22 Sanhedrin 109b

and satirically of judges who distinguish between law and morals.

The four judges of Sodom[23], they say, were known as Shakrai, Shakurai, Zayyafi and Mazledina, symbolic names meaning Liar, Awful Liar, Forger and Perverter of Justice. A witty legend tells of Eliezer the servant of Abraham who arrived in Sodom and was attacked and wounded. He appeared before the local judge who said to him, "Pay the attacker for letting your blood." He thereupon hurled a stone at the judge, who had addressed him, and injured him. The judge cried in astonishment. Eliezer said to him, "The reward you owe me for letting your blood give to my attacker".

A famous Sage disparaged judges who resorted to compromise in cases where they did not establish the law. He called them "compromise judges".[24]

Jewish law insists on the independence of the judges. Although the final decision is that of the majority, each judge is enjoined to retain his independent opinion, whether he concurs with the majority or the minority. He must not allow himself to be influenced in his final decision of the opinion of another judge, however renowned for his legal learning and forensic skill. The Tosefta[25] states: "Do not say at the time of the decision 'It is proper for a servant to be like his master'; say what is in your own mind". Similarly, "Do not say 'It is sufficient

23 Ibid.
24 Baba Bathra 133b; Rashi says: "Compromise judges" who are not proficient in the law. They resort to 50% award to each party on the basis of "money in doubt". Rabbenu Ḥananel explains דחצצתא as "of the cemetery", perhaps "judges of the cemetery", those for whom the law is not living.
25 Sanhedrin 3,8

that I vote like the other judge', rather state your own opinion".[26]

In the sources, a Scriptural text is cited in support of the Sages' view. "Neither shall you bear witness in a cause to incline after the many to change judgment".[27] This is interpreted to mean that the individual judge should always endeavour to arrive at an independent decision.[28]

The judge must be fearless in his pursuit of justice. He must not be arrogant. He must be the embodiment of integrity and rectitude. A judge must never reason that since the decision of the majority is binding he might as well support it. He must state his opinion clearly even if he knows that it will not be accepted. Once, however, the majority decision has been reached every judge, even if he held a minority opinion, is duty bound to submit to the decision of the majority. With delicacy of touch the Sages paid the true judge the high compliment of being God's collaborator.[29]

That the judges were generally fully sensitive to their great responsibilities is evident from the Talmudic sources. Two famous Sages, Rab and Rava, feared lest they might err in their judgment.[30] They offered up a prayer asking that they might be as free from sin at the end of a case as they were at its beginning. In their humility they were concerned that they did not perhaps possess the high qualities listed in the Torah.[31] The attitude of the Sages towards prejudiced judges is

---

26 Mechilta De Rab Shimon, Exodus 23,2
27 Exodus 23,2
28 Maimonides: Sanhedrin 10,1; Sefer Ha-Ḥinuch 77
29 Shabbath 10a
30 Yoma 86b, 87a
31 Exodus 18,21

reflected in a solemn utterance.[32] "The sword comes to the world for the suppression or delay of justice and for the perversion of justice, and on account of those who misinterpret the Torah".[33]

The Talmud holds prejudiced judges responsible for all the ills in the world.[34] For society must be built on justice and righteousness and the judge has a vital role to play in it. He must interpret and apply the law according to the ethical concepts and moral principles that underlie the law. Law and morality form an indivisible unity.

The Torah embraces justice and righteousness as well as love and kindness. Thus 'law', which is often its translation, does not convey the meaning of Torah. Torah is a code of conduct, a compelling guide and inspiring force in life.

The Psalmist spoke rapturously of the Torah.[35] Rab's teaching is apt. The commandments have been given for the purpose of refining man's character and conduct.[36]

To what extent the judge is to follow slavishly the law or statute is an old question dealt with in jurisprudence. The Jewish legal maxim known as שודא דדייני "a decision at the discretion of the judges" allows a judge to follow, in particular cases, his own assessment. The following case is instructive. If one bequeathed his property to one named Tobiah and two men of the same name - and both are scholars and related to the testator - claimed a right to the legacy, the decision is left to the discretion of the judges. Rashi holds that it is up to the judges to determine

32 Yebamoth 109b; Sanhedrin 7a
33 Aboth 5,11
34 Shabbath 139a
35 Psalm 119,97-104
36 Genesis Rabbah 44,1

judiciously whom the donor had in mind.[37] In doing so they would consider the character and moral qualities for whose benefit the deceased intended his bequest. Some authorities were of the opinion that the restriction of the principle of "judicial discretion" was necessary as it might lead to arbitrary decisions.

Rabbenu Tam says that traditionally the principle of "judicial discretion" applied to real estate but not to chattels and could only be practised by a distinguished scholar.[38]

The Rabbis referred to the ideal judge as the judge who delivers "true judgment" הדן דין אמת לאמתו. Perhaps the words bear another meaning. The judge who decides according to the letter of the law may be described as one who "judges truly" דין אמת. But he who decides according to the spirit of the higher law of morality refers to a judge who gives a profoundly true judgment.[39] הדן דין אמת לאמתו.

The Rabbis detected in the Biblical injunction "thou shalt not revile God"[40] also a prohibition against reviling a judge. That judges were liable to be criticized by discontented parties is evident from the following incident. Two litigants, they tell, came before a judge who found for the plaintiff. The successful party went forth and said, "There is none like this judge". The man appeared in another case before the same judge who decided against him. The disappointed litigant then said, "There is no other judge as foolish as this judge". A man said to him, "Yesterday the judge was praiseworthy,

37 Ketuboth 85b
38 Ibid. 94b, Tosafoth
39 Megillah 15b, Tosafoth, cf. Baba Bathra 8b
40 Exodus 22,27

today he is foolish?" Therefore the Torah enjoins, "Thou shalt not revile a judge".[41]

Divergent opinions among judges were resolved in compliance with the majority vote. The Mishnah records the opinions of the majority as well as those of individual scholars. While the Halachah is generally decided in accordance with the views held by the School of Hillel those of the School of Shammai are also stated. Even when the decision was according to neither School,[42] their respective opinions were recorded. "To teach future generations that none should persist in his opinion, as the Fathers of the World did not persist in their opinion". It is perhaps possible to suggest another reason. Interpretations of the Rabbis, even if not accepted as law, are a contribution to Torah knowledge.[43] Indeed, the opinion of the minority, whilst not binding in law, may afford a perceptive insight into a legal concept. If preserved in writing or orally, it may be considered by others when dealing with the same or similar problems.[44]

The Mishnah explains: [45]"Why do they record the opinion of an individual against that of the majority, seeing that the Halachah is decided in accordance with the opinion of the majority? So that another or later court may know the decision and the authority, since no court can revoke the decision of another court, unless it exceeds the latter both in wisdom and number. If it exceeds in wisdom but not in number, or in number but not in wisdom, it cannot revoke the decision". The Mishnah,[46]

41   Exodus Rabbah 31,8
42   M. Eduyoth 1,1-4
43   Ibid. 1,6
44   Encyclopaedia Talmudith vol. IX p.261
45   Eduyoth 1,5
46   Ibid. 1,6

it has been explained, intended to emphasize that the opinion of the dissenting individual, if sound, is never lost. The majority of a later court may reach a decision in harmony with the dissenting individual or an earlier court. Indeed, a court may, in particular circumstances, decide in accordance with a minority opinion.

Court composition and procedure are part of most legal systems. The procedure prescribed in Jewish law for civil cases, as we have seen, bears testimony to a profound concern for justice.[47] According to the Bible cases involving indebtedness could be decided by one judge, as it is written: "Thou shalt judge thy fellow with righteousness".[48] The injunction is in the singular. The Sages, however, as already mentioned, ordained that these cases should be heard by three judges. But as a court of three might sometimes be difficult to convene and this would tend to discourage likely creditors the rule was relaxed. Behind the lenient view there was clearly the concept of humanity and a profound awareness of the need for new procedural rules in changed circumstances.[49]

R. Ishmael said, "Do not judge alone, for none may judge alone except One (God); do not say to your co-judges, 'accept my view' for they (who are in the majority) are entitled to say that, but not you".[50] In litigation it is not safe for the judge to rely on himself alone, regardless of his knowledge, competence and judicial experience. He should share the wisdom, learning and experience of others. Moreover, a judge must not force his opinions

47 Aboth 4,10
48 Leviticus 19,15
49 Sanhedrin 3a
50 Aboth 4,10

upon his colleagues. For they are as competent to judge as he is and theirs is the majority view.

Nowhere is the power and authority of the Jewish courts reflected more forcefully than in the halachic maxim הפקר בית דין הפקר. It gives the court the power to dispossess an individual of his property. The Biblical basis for this legal rule is traced back to Ezra. In order to stem the tide of assimilation that threatened to undermine the religious life and loyalties of many of those who had returned to Palestine from the Babylonian captivity during the first days of the Second Common-wealth, Ezra ordered all those who had come back to appear before him and his colleagues for admonition and directive. Those who failed to answer his summons were to be punished by having "their substance expropriated and themselves separated from the congregation of the captivity".[51]

As for the power of the court it is important to consider the statement of R. Eliezer b. Jacob. He said "I have heard from my teachers that the Beth Din may (when necessary) impose flagellation and pronounce capital sentences even when not warranted by the Torah. Yet not with the intention of disregarding the Torah but, on the contrary, in order to make a fence round it"[52]

It has been suggested that the judges were invested with great power and high judicial authority.[53] The Codes and Responsa literature contain many references to this wide-ranging and potent power of the judges. Some scholars hold that the rule of הפקר בית דין הפקר was applied only

51 Ezra 10,7-8
52 Sanhedrin 46a

שמעתי שב"ד מכין ועונשין שלא מן התורה ולא לעבור על דברי תורה אלא
לעשות סייג לתורה

53 Deuteronomy 17,12-13 cf. Sanhedrin 89a

as a precautionary and protective measure. They cite the *prozbul* as an example. Similarly, in matters social and ritual which involved material ownership of an individual the Rabbis would, in given situations, resort to this right in order to protect an individual or a community against transgressing a Torah precept. Others held that the maxim was applied by the court in cases where it was proper and essential so to do. It has been suggested that the power of the court to declare a person's property ownerless derives from the sovereignty and authority that the court enjoys.[54]

Regarding the administration of justice two contrasting attitudes of the Rabbis are recorded in the Talmud. One requires the judge to act always in accordance with strict justice whilst the other urges the judge to follow the path of peace and harmony even if it involves compromise by the agreement of the parties concerned. In other words it is the task and duty of the court to try and arbitrate. According to one rabbinical opinion unless the litigants themselves ask the court to arbitrate, the court must not suggest this procedure. Another view permitted the court, even stressed its duty, to persuade the litigants to agree to a פשרה, a compromise, which also pays due regard to the law. In this way both justice and equity will be served, hardship will be avoided and peace will be promoted. If, however, the parties insist on strict justice, it is the duty of the court to adhere to their wishes. Litigants who agree to arbitration may change their minds and ask for a decision in accordance with strict justice. If they seal their agreement with a קנין, a "legal form of acceptance", by which a verbal agreement becomes binding, this "form of acceptance" obliges them

---

54 Ezra 10,7-8

to obey the decision of the judges even though it does not conform to strict justice.[55]

The Bible strongly enjoins deliberation in judgment. "Was ever such a crime committed since the Israelites left Egypt? Think of it and decide what is to be done".[56] Careful deliberation was imperative at all times and especially in dispute and conflict.

The men of the "Great Assembly", who were the religious and political leaders of the Jewish people in an age of great moment in its history, gave expression to their thinking when they called for patient, careful and long deliberation in judgment.[57] Wisdom, judicial and judicious perception are crucial and fundamental in the administration of justice.

"Legal decisions", the Sages declared, "required a mind as clear as the North wind".[58] The North wind made the day clear, whereas a day of a strong South wind made the day dull which was not conducive to clear thinking. A famous judge, we are told, would not hear cases on a day of a strong South wind.[59] Maimonides[60] says that if a judge can arbitrate between the contending parties he is praiseworthy. If he is unsuccessful in his endeavour to arbitrate and conciliate he should give his judgment with calm and deliberation.

I have referred to court procedure. Jewish judges could impose various forms of punishment. That imprisonment in some cases preceded the trial is evident from two incidents mentioned in the Torah. We are told of a

55 S.A.Ḥ.M. 12,7
56 Judges 19,30
57 Aboth 1,1
58 Megillah 28b
59 Erubin 65a; Rashi ad loc
60 Introduction to Seder Zeraim

blasphemer who was the son of an Israelitish woman.[61] He was imprisoned pending judgment. The Torah ordained: "Thou shalt not revile God"[62] but no penalty for the violation of the injunction had been stated. It was, therefore, necessary to ascertain the proper penalty and Moses inquired of God. The blasphemer was imprisoned while awaiting the Divine answer.

The second incident involved a man who had desecrated the Sabbath.[63] His sin was wilful. In Jewish law the public violation of the Sabbath was regarded with the same rigour as idolatry, which was deemed a revolt against God. Sabbath-breaking was a capital offence and the law had been made known in the Torah, but not the method of execution. Pending declaration of the manner of execution, the Sabbath-breaker, we are told, was imprisoned. These two incidents, tradition relates, were contemporaneous but the offenders were not incarcerated together.

There was, according to a Rabbinic source, a special cell for those condemned to death.[64] Support for the view that the two offenders were not imprisoned together is indicated by the Hebrew words used in each case. Rashi detected in the words "and they put him", relating to the Sabbath-breaker, that he was held by himself in a special cell as the penalty laid down in his case was death. The law in the case of the blasphemer had not been made known and if he were held together with the Sabbath-breaker who was under sentence of death, it would cause him additional anguish and pain. His offence, he might think, would be similarly punished.

61 Leviticus 24,10ff.
62 Exodus 22,27
63 Numbers 15,32ff.
64 Sifra Leviticus, 24, 10ff

In considering the question of punishment it is significant that in the Torah we find but few references to sentences of imprisonment. It is generally held that punishment has more than one purpose. Indeed, the reform of the prisoner, the protection of the public from his future misdeeds and depradations and the deterrence of him and others from committing similar crimes — these are some of the purposes of punishment. In addition to these there is the deprivation of the criminal's freedom which also serves to prevent the prisoner from becoming a danger. There are still other objectives: retribution and the public expression of anger and outrage at the commission of a grave crime.

While English law distinguishes between crime and sin there is hardly such a distinction to be found in Jewish law. For in Judaism, transgression against the Divine law or against the principles of morality is in defiance of God's will.

"Lest thy brother be dishonoured before thine eyes".[65] After the offender had received his punishment he is referred to as "thy brother". Even if he has committed a criminal act his human dignity must be respected and he is to be received again into the fellowship of Israel.

It would appear that in Jewish law punishment has a moral objective, the restoration of the criminal to a good life and right conduct. It, indeed, reflects the attitude of Judaism to the weak and the fallen.[66] The idea of punishment as retribution designed to inflict torment and humiliation is alien to Jewish legal notions.

After a man was found guilty and was liable to flogging, the lashing had to be carried out in the presence

65 Deuteronomy 25,2
66 Isaiah 55,7

of the judge as a safeguard against harsh application of the punishment.[67] When stripes were administered due regard was to be paid to the physical condition of the offender.[68] While the Torah mentions forty lashes the Rabbis interpreted the number to mean closely connected with forty or not to exceed forty. In practice thirty-nine was the maximum.[69]

Persons who were condemned to death were given certain incense in wine in order to intoxicate them. This was the task undertaken by the noble ladies of Jerusalem, a sensitive example of *noblesse oblige*.[70]

Indeed, the Halachah applied the Golden Rule[71] also to the enemies of society, to the sinner and the criminal and even to those who were guilty of murder. Their sentence had to be carried out with consideration and compassion. They were to be given a gentle death. Justice had to go hand in hand with mercy and humanity. Where there is conflict between social justice and morality the latter must take precedence.[72] Of particular interest is the passage[73] which tells of the manner in which the witnesses in a capital case were addressed by the court. It was the duty of the court to draw the attention of the witnesses not only to the sanctity of life of the individual involved but also to that of the generations yet unborn.

This high concept of the value of human life, that each individual represents the potential of an entire world, suggests an unique notion of humanity. However, the

---

67 Deuteronomy 25,2-3
68 Ibid.
69 Makkoth 22a-b
70 Sanhedrin 43a
71 Leviticus 19,18
72 Pesaḥim 35a; Nedarim 65b
73 Sanhedrin 37a

enormity of capital cases and the attendant procedure had to be divorced from emotional considerations. The dictum of R. Akiba[74] "we may not show pity in a civil suit" is a juristic principle which equally applies to criminal cases. The Rabbis were humane but not sentimental. In order to eradicate evil from society even the virtue of pity must not affect justice.

In defiance of the Divine instructions King Saul showed clemency to Agag, king of the Amalekites.[75] For arrogating to himself the right to decide how far he should fulfil God's behest he was punished. In his confession he declares his weakness. The comment of the Sages is equally significant.[76]

That Jewish law attaches responsibility for crime not only to its perpetrators but also imposes a duty on those who could have possibly prevented it may be seen from the Biblical law which enjoined on the elders of a city, in whose vicinity a slain victim has been found, to wash their hands over an atonement offering and declare: "Our hands have not shed this blood neither have our eyes seen it".[77]

In Judaism murder is not only a crime against the victim but also a sin against God in whose image man was made. When the murderer was unknown the whole community, as it were, shared responsibility for the crime committed against one of its members.

The Sages add their own characteristic comment. Surely, they say, no one could suspect the elders of the community of having committed the crime? But by their

74 Ketuboth 84a
75 I Samuel 15,9-24
76 Yoma 22b
77 Deuteronomy 21,1-9

statement they avowed that they did not neglect the victim. He did not come to them hungry and they failed to give him food. He did not come to them friendless and they failed to befriend him. Thus the Sages emphasized the great principle of corporate responsibility.[78] The act of mercy performed by the public-spirited women of Jerusalem, referred to above, was perhaps to demonstrate likewise that the community as such felt a sense of guilt for the crime. The women, who were clearly more sensitive, took this compassionate task upon themselves.[79]

It is informative that circumstantial evidence is not admissible in Jewish law. The Rabbis based this rule on the Biblical precept. "At the mouth of two witnesses, or three witnesses, shall he that is to die be put to death; at the mouth of one witness he shall not be be put to death".[80] A Talmudic passage quoting an actual case is illuminating. It is reported in the name of Simeon b. Shetah. He once saw a man pursuing another into a cave. Simeon followed him and saw him emerging from the cave holding in his hand a sword dripping with blood. He also saw the victim in the cave with convulsions. While the Sage was sure that the pursuer was the murderer he could not convict him as the law demanded the testimony of two credible witnesses as well as witnesses who had warned the offender.[81]

The sources record another example of the testimony of two witnesses that was also rejected by the court in harmony with the opinion of the latter Sage. "We saw," the witnesses said, "the accused with a sword in his hand run after a man; the man who was pursued escaped into a

---

78 Sifre Deuteronomy 21
79 Yoma 22b; Sanhedrin 43a
80 Deuteronomy 17,6
81 Tosefta Sanhedrin 8,2

shop. The pursuer entered the shop after him; there we saw the slain man struggle and the sword, dripping with blood, in the hand of the alleged murderer." No charge could be sustained and no punishment imposed unless the actual commission of the crime was seen by two eye witnesses and "warning witnesses". If, however, one was known to have committed murder but there were no valid witnesses he was imprisoned for life and was fed with a prison diet consisting of scant bread and scant water.[82]

Concerning the question of a man's confession or admission the Rabbis ruled that in civil cases the "admission of the defendant is as valid as the testimony of a hundred witnesses."[83] In capital cases the confession of the accused is of no legal validity. The Talmudic dictum "a man cannot incriminate himself" אין אדם משים עצמו רשע is applied.[84] It is held that this is biblically ordained.

The following examples will illustrate the respective attitudes. If a man says that he owes another man one hundred *zuz* he is legally bound to make payment of the amount, but if a man confesses that he gave false testimony, or had committed any other crime for which he is punishable by a fine, stripes or death, his confession is not accepted as evidence. He is not punished for the offence to which he confesses. Various explanations have been suggested. A person's evidence against himself has no legal validity because, just as close relatives are in Jewish law disqualified as witnesses, there can be no closer relationship than self.[85] Some held that self-incrimination was not admissible as evidence because

---

82   Sanhedrin 37b. Ibid. 81b; cf. I Kings 22,27; Isaiah 30,20
83   Tosefta Baba Metzia 1,6; Maimonides: Eduth 12,2
84   Sanhedrin 9,b; Yebamoth 25b; Maimonides: Eduth 12,2
85   S.A.H.M. 33,10

man, having been created in the image of God, cannot himself deny his natural attribute of decency and dignity with which he is endowed at birth.[86]

Maimonides suggests the following rationalisation of this rabbinic principle. He writes: "The Sanhedrin inflicted neither capital punishment nor flagellation upon one who confessed to having committed a crime. It is possible that his mind was confused. Perhaps he is a person, bitter of soul, troubled and distressed, who looks forward to death. He may have a suicidal tendency. Perhaps it was for this reason that he confesses to a crime which he did not commit".[87] While as a physician Maimonides no doubt knew of cases of suicide or attempted suicide due to deep depression and despair he held that the principle regarding self-incrimination was a Divine decree. But this did not prevent him from suggesting a psychological reason for the legal principle.[88]

Another explanation has been advanced. Every man standing trial is to be deemed innocent until his guilt is proved. While other systems of law accept confession as evidence, this is in conflict with the need of proof to establish guilt. Where self-incrimination is accepted the person's guilt is admitted regardless of the trial and its proceedings. Jewish law,[89] however, insists on independent evidence of guilt or innocence.

It is interesting that in the opinion of the Rabbis while

86 Sanhedrin 37a; Maimonides: Sanhedrin 12,3 and 18,6 and Commentaries
87 Sanhedrin 9b; Maimonides: Eduth 12,2; S.A.H.M. 34,28
88 Sanhedrin 9,1-4
89 Some held that the self-incriminating was subject to excommunication on his own evidence. M. Sanhedrin 6,2; Meiri ad loc. Others were opposed to this view: Knesseth Hagedolah in the name of the Rosh.

self-incrimination had no legal validity and did not disqualify a man as a witness it would not preclude him from taking an oath that would absolve him from payment. This attitude reflects the human insight of the Sages. Despite his self-condemnation continuing credibility might help him to repent and receive forgiveness from the Heavenly Court for his lapse.

The methods followed in some countries in our times in order to obtain confessions from an accused would not be allowed in Jewish law. Confession, voluntary or obtained by pressure, is excluded on the ground that "no man may incriminate himself". There is growing concern in some modern countries relating to convictions based on evidence obtained under pressure. Some rules provide in English law for the exclusion of evidence obtained improperly and unfairly.

From a close survey of the Talmudic sources it can be seen that capital punishment was rarely carried out and that it was a law in theory rather than in practice. Indeed, the Sages declared, "A court that convicts one man in seven years is called a destructive court. R. Eleazar b. Azariah says one in even seventy years".[90]

It is clear that the reason for the Rabbis' attitude was because in Judaism punishment was designed neither as retribution nor as a deterrent. Its purpose was to teach the people that criminal conduct was a sin against God and man. The procedure of the courts in capital cases supports our suggestion. Witnesses in such charges were brought in and seriously warned. They were urged to reflect that capital cases are not like monetary cases. In civil suits it is possible to correct an error of fact or judgment by making material restitution, but in capital

90 M. Makkoth 1,10

cases the witnesses were held responsible for the blood of the accused and for the blood of his descendants. The Sages cite the case of Cain who killed his brother, concerning whom it is written, "The bloods of thy brother cry unto me"; the plural 'bloods' suggests his blood and the blood of his descendants.[91] Punishment is not retribution because no person is able to assess whether the punishment is equal to the crime. Human fallibility may cause the judge to err and the death of the murderer would not be that of an individual but of generations. Indeed, the warning administered to the witnesses could equally apply to the judge. The purpose of punishment was moral and was to lead to remorse and repentance.

"Forty years", the Talmud declares, "before the destruction of the Second Temple the laws relating to capital cases were suspended because the Sanhedrin had been exiled and were no longer in their place in the Temple."[92]

The attitude to the homicide in Judaism also reflects a most humane approach. The Torah enjoins that six Cities of Refuge, three on either side of the Jordan, were to be set aside as places of asylum for accidental homicide.[93] Others could be substituted provided they conformed to the rules laid down concerning distance and geographical position. Forty-two cities allotted to the Levites could also serve as Cities of Refuge.[94] Various reasons have been advanced for the institution of the Cities of Refuge.[95] They served as a protection for the man-slayer

91 Sanhedrin 37a
92 Shabbath 15a
93 Numbers 35,6ff; Joshua 21, 13-40; I Chronicles 6,39ff
94 Numbers 35,6ff; Makkoth 12a-13a; Maimonides: Rotzeaḥ, 8,9
95 Numbers 35,25ff; Makkoth 10a

against any attack upon him by a near relative of the victim described as the "avenger of blood". The use of the Hebrew verb meaning "to flee" — to the Cities of Refuge — supports this explanation. Another reason given for the Cities of Refuge suggests that exile was regarded as a form of punishment. The Torah emphasized that the homicide could not escape the punishment of exile. Like murder his crime could not be commuted by the payment of a ransom.[96]

The duration of the stay of the exiled homicide being linked with the life of the High Priest has prompted yet another explanation. The City of Refuge to which the homicide was exiled served as a fitting place for atonement which, according to a Talmudic sentiment, is more easily achieved through exile. Maimonides stresses that the social, educational and cultural needs of the convicted had to be provided for. The provisions set out in his Code[97] clearly do not support the notion of punishment. Nor has punishment in the Jewish concept the objective to deprive the offender of his physical or mental freedom. It has a moral purpose. The homicide was not to be imprisoned in some desolate place but among those who might help him to repent and reform.[98] True repentance must be in thought as well as in deed. Maimonides also emphasizes that the Cities of Refuge were for the protection of homicides against the fury of the "avengers of blood".[99]

The width of the roads leading to the Cities of Refuge was generously prescribed. The roads were to be thirty-two cubits wide in order to afford fugitives every facility

96 Numbers 35,31
97 Rotzeaḥ, Chapters 7-8
98 Isaiah 55,7
99 Guide III, 40

from all directions to reach a City of Refuge, where they would enjoy sanctuary.[100] In addition there were to be sign-posts bearing the inscription "to the City of Refuge" at every crossroad indicating the direction of the particular City of Refuge.[101] If the courts were negligent in ensuring the prescribed width of the roads leading to the Cities of Refuge, they would be regarded, according to Maimonides, as being guilty of bloodshed.[102]

The Sefer Ha-Hinuch while giving several reasons for the Cities of Refuge emphasizes the aspect of punishment. "Because of the enormity of killing which is destructive of society the Rabbis declared that he who commits murder even if he has performed all the commandments does not escape punishment".[103]

Again, he who is guilty of homicide since he caused such a serious mishap should suffer exile and isolation from his family and friends. The company of total strangers could in itself constitute harsh punishment. The Cities of Refuge served a further beneficial purpose. The relatives of the victim would not face the man-slayer. It was a deeply human consideration. For, "all the ways of the Torah are pleasantness and all her paths are peace".[104]

I have been discussing the moral and ethical values that underlie some concepts of Jewish law. But the Talmudic ruling כל דאלים גבר "the stronger is to prevail," applicable in certain cases, is in seeming conflict with those basic principles. To cite but one or two examples: "If there are two claimants to a property and

100 Baba Bathra 100b
101 Tosefta Makkoth 3,5; Makkoth 10b
102 Rotzeah 8,6
103 On Numbers 35,25 No. 410
104 Proverbs 3,17

one says 'It belongs to my father' while the other says 'to my father', neither of them producing any evidence, R. Naḥman says that the stronger of the two prevails.[105] The opinion of R. Naḥman has puzzled the commentators. According to the Rosh, this ruling is based upon the influence of conscience upon man's actions. The ruling was in the nature of a test. The wrongful party would be reluctant to take possession of the property lest his opponent may later produce conclusive evidence that will deprive him of his ill-gotten gain. Indeed, the Rosh held that the party who has right on his side and has taken possession is likely ultimately to find evidence in support of his claim. Other authorities did not share the view of the Rosh and sought to limit the force of this ruling which they considered alien to the concept of justice and equity.[106] Furthermore, the Rosh contends that the conscience of the side whose claim is either false or uncertain will finally weaken in his position. While the attitude of the Rosh testifies to his belief in the high moral conscience of every Jew, the Talmudic dictum seems to suggest that the party that has a stronger case will ultimately succeed in establishing his claim. If one of the parties seized the property in accordance with the ruling of R. Naḥman, the opponent can, the Tur held, impose on him an oath. His action does not decide finally the question of right. The determining factor must be the oath which is a legal institution and therefore binding. The later authorities sought to lessen the force of what seemed so strange a ruling.[107]

Another case cited relates to brothers or partners who divide a field among themselves. If one claims as his

---

105 Baba Bathra 34b
106 Rosh ad loc; S.A.Ḥ.M. 139
107 S.A.Ḥ.M. 139 and Commentaries

portion that which adjoins his own field, we apply, according to one authority, the rule of בר מצרא. The Sma is of the opinion that in such cases they must first cast lots and only if the one who claims the right of בר מצרא loses, then we apply "he who is stronger prevails".[108] Significantly one of the later authorities wished to abolish the Talmudic rule on moral grounds. He writes: "I feel impelled to say that in these times it is very doubtful whether one should decide according to the Talmudic principle. Furthermore, the reason (suggested by the Rosh) that he who has right on his side will do his utmost to establish his claim does not apply in our days. There are many who risk their lives to establish wrong claims. Therefore, where it is not possible to divide the property in dispute it should be dealt with as in the case of *mizranut* and lots are to be cast. And although this is a new decision yet the need of the hour dictates it. He is certain that his masters and colleagues will concur".[109]

It has been suggested that the ruling was intended as a procedural expedient designed to adjourn the case. In postponing judgment the party with right on his side will ultimately succeed in producing convincing evidence where such evidence exists. Confidence and conviction in a just and fair claim will sustain the party in his efforts to establish a lawful right to the property in dispute. The court decides in accordance with the ruling of R. Naḥman, to adjourn the case *sine die*.

The question of judicial precedent merits careful consideration. In the English legal system an actual case may constitute an authoritative source. Thus the final

108   See Mordecai Baba Bathra end of Ch. 1; Baba Bathra 35a S.A.Ḥ.M.
      174 Rema; cf. Rabbi Dr. S. Federbusch, Hamusar Ve Hamishpat be-
      Yisrael p.158.
109   Shevuth Yaakov on Ḥ.M. No. 162

conclusion that flows from the judgment often serves as a precedent for other cases. In Jewish law precedent is respected but the final decision is based on principles. In the Talmud the conduct of a certain Sage in a given case is often quoted as a decision.[110] Such decisions could serve as precedents in both ritual laws and in monetary cases. Whilst the Jewish judges would naturally study earlier judgments they were not bound by them.

The finality of judgment implied in *res judicata* is not compatible with Jewish law. Perhaps the humanity that distinguishes Jewish law would not favour such rigidity. If after a court decision has been given one of the parties produces a new piece of evidence, the case has to be heard again and a new decision given.

In discussing the place of precedent in Jewish law it remains to be added that the example and action of an acknowledged halachic authority would serve as a precedent to be followed. For he is the embodiment of the law, and his action serves as a reliable guide.

In the Jewish legal system, as has been observed, justice and equity form the supreme principle assuring order, peace and harmony among men. Not only in personal relations, but in all human issues, national, political and economic, it must be the basis and substance. When the force of justice and righteousness will hold sway in society, universal peace and security will be established. So we have been promised long ago: "And the work of justice shall be peace and the effect of justice quietness and confidence".[111]

110 M. Berakoth 1,1
111 Isaiah 32, 17

CHAPTER FOUR

FAMILY LAW

The family is the most important social institution. It has been the strongest stabilizing factor in society. Perhaps more than anything else it has generated integrity and loyalties in the home. In Judaism the self-sufficiency, dignity and sanctity of the family have added lustre to life with parents being respected and admired; with the father held in high regard and affection; with the mother being loved and honoured and with the children being shown a tender solicitude. The family provided the ideal background for justice and moral lessons. Most significantly the laws of family life constitute no less than one fourth of the entire Code of Jewish law. The high Jewish concept of the family is reflected in the many legal rulings, enactments and ordinances.

The institution of marriage, upon which the family rests, received full and interesting attention in the Halachah. Concerning marriage the Bible says: "And the Lord God said: It is not good that man should be alone; I will make him a helpmeet for him".[1] Nowhere is the doctrine of the sacredness of the human personality more

---

1 Genesis 2,18

vividly reflected than in the Jewish view of marriage. In Judaism, marriage is based on the ideal of love and tenderness and the beauty of holiness. Marriage in the Jewish tradition is a sacred covenant which implies permanence, fidelity and unimpeachable loyalty. In the marriage relationship religion and spirituality must play a prominent part. "When a husband and wife have merit", say the Rabbis, "God's presence will be found in their midst".[2]

A brief comment expresses tellingly the Rabbis' concern for the welfare and dignity of women. "The Sages were considerate towards the daughters of Israel".[3] The Rabbis condemned those who married for money.[4] "The money which a man takes with his wife is not money acquired equitably. Anyone who does so is regarded as if he took his wife because of her money".[5] "The acceptance by the bridegroom of a dowry," writes a rabbinical figure of our own times, "is something of which the Rabbis do not approve, as he appears to marry his wife for her material possessions. That the religious leaders permitted the practice was on account of the difficult times. It became a general custom to promise a dowry to the bridegroom in order to enable him to eke out a living for himself and his family. A livelihood had become difficult owing to the pressures of the times. It required capital. Some deducted a third of the dowry promised so that the man does not appear to marry for money".[6]

This liberal sentiment runs through the many rulings

2 Sotah 17a
3 Ketuboth 2a
4 Kiddushin 70a
5 S.A.E.H. 2,1 Rema
6 Rabbi Aaron Lewin, Responsa: "Avne Hefetz" No. 11

and enactments in regard to the Jewish woman. One example will serve. Women were permitted to anoint themselves on the Sabbath because they were used to it. "All daughters of Israel", says the Code, "are like princesses."[7]

To cement the bonds of love and understanding between husband and wife the Torah provided that during the first year of marriage no public duties devolved upon the husband. He was exempted from military service in time of war. He was to cheer his wife.[8] It was clearly deemed crucial for the married couple to spend all their leisure together in order to adjust to each other in their new relationship.

The Rabbis interpreted the Biblical injunction generously. Not only was the husband exempt during the first year of marriage from war service, but also from non-combative duties such as supplying food and drink for the army and repairing the roads. War in this connection refers to מלחמת רשות "a voluntary war". He was to remain at home with his wife. But in the case of mandatory war, all were obliged to serve in the armed forces, even the newly-wed couple.[9] Maimonides says the husband shall be free from any kind of service both military and civil, imposed by the State.[10]

That polygamy was but rarely practised is evident from many sources. In Midrashic literature, which reflects conditions of life, social, religious and moral, the attitude to polygamy was strongly critical. In commenting on the words of I Samuel 1,2 "And he (Elkanah) had two

7   Baba Kamma 82a; Baba Bathra 22a
8   Deuteronomy 24,5
9   Sotah 44b
10 Sefer Hamitzvoth 311; Sefer HaḤinuch 582

wives", the Midrash says that the words indicate disapproval.[11]

Indeed, polygamy which was frowned upon among Jews in Talmudic and later times shows the regard Jews had for the status and dignity of women. According to an old tradition Boaz first declined to perform the duty of a kinsman to acquire the estate of Ruth's husband and to marry her on the ground that he was married and he could not bring in another woman. [12]

A Talmudic Rabbi ruled that a man who marries a second wife should divorce his first wife and pay her the marriage settlement.[13] The ban of Rabbenu Gershom, which was clearly designed to make the woman's life easier and to avoid strife and tension in the home and family, forbade polygamy for Ashkenazic Jews. Permission could be granted to a husband to take another wife only in special circumstances. But such permission, even in cases of extreme necessity, would require the approbation of one hundred rabbis representing three different countries. Other conditions, too, govern such permission — all intended to protect the interests of women. Indeed, sanction to marry a second wife was extremely difficult to obtain.[14]

Another example of the Rabbis' consideration for women is contained in an incident recorded in the Jerusalem Talmud.[15] A man of meagre means, desirous of improving his social and financial position, had won the heart of a wealthy woman. He had been promised a large dowry. When the time for the wedding arrived, the

11 Yalkut Shimeoni on 1 Samuel 77
12 Targum on Ruth 4,6
13 Yebamoth 65a
14 S.A.E.H. 1,10
15 J. Ketuboth 13,5

bride's father refused to keep his promise. The man, unable to realize his ambition, declined to proceed with the marriage. According to ancient Palestinian custom, betrothal, which ceremony had taken place in this case, bound the couple. A divorce was essential to dissolve the betrothal. But the man refused to release her by divorce in accordance with the law. The woman appealed to Admon for redress claiming that the man either release her or marry her. Some authorities were of the opinion that the man had been the victim of a fraudulent contract, but Admon, no doubt out of concern for the woman in her plight, ruled in her favour.[16]

The case of an orphan girl, whose marriage was delayed on a Friday owing to difficulties and last minute negotiations relating to a dowry promised, will serve as a later example of the Rabbis' solicitude for a young woman. The decision of the Rema in the matter bears quoting. A girl in Cracow was promised a dowry by her father on her engagement. The father died after the engagement and the girl, who also had no mother, was taken care of by her uncle. The marriage was fixed for a Friday, by which day all the preparations were complete. But as the promised dowry was not forthcoming, the bridegroom refused to go on with the marriage. The parties submitted the matter to arbitration, and after lengthy negotiations a settlement was agreed. It was long after the commencement of the Sabbath. The Rema, against accepted practice, solemnized the marriage in order to obviate any new complications that could arise from further delay. The Rema's bold action provoked strong criticism from other Rabbis. But he remained firm in defending his position. "In such and similar

16 Ibid. and Ketuboth 105a

circumstances," Isserls writes with emotion and conviction, "he who inclines towards the more lenient view is not the loser". An eye-witness, R. Menaḥem b. Isaac of Tiktin, a disciple of the Rema, in recording independently this incident adds: "And the Master delayed the Friday Evening Service in his Synagogue until the marriage ceremony was performed". Few will fail to be impressed by the deep concern for the happiness of a bride, who had already suffered humiliation, shown by the famous sixteenth century Halachist. The joy of the bride justified, in his view, delay in the welcome of Bride Sabbath.[17]

While marriage in Judaism presupposes a life-long relationship that binds the parties naturally and legally, yet when a marriage is irretrievably undermined, divorce is the remedy. Judaism does not insist on the indissolubility of marriage. Indeed, in the Torah divorce is referred to as an institution which alone can dissolve a marriage.[18]

A man may not remarry his wife if her second husband divorced her or died.[19] A Cohen may not marry a divorced woman nor may he remarry his former wife.[20]

That the Rabbis considered divorce a tragedy is evident from the emotive way in which they speak of the dissolution of a first marriage.[21]

The Talmud, the Codes and the Responsa literature

---

17   Isserls: Responsa 125; Betzah 36b; Bet Yosef O.Ḥ. 339 cf: Ḥiddushe Anshe Shem on Mordecai (end of Betzah); See M.S. Lew, The Jews of Poland pp 33-34

18   Deuteronomy 24, 1-3

19   Ibid. 4

20   Leviticus 21,7

21   Gittin 90b כל המגרש אשתו ראשונה אפילו מזבח מוריד עליו דמעות; See Dr. Samuel Daiches, Essays and Address pages 92-93

devote a great deal of discussion and detail to the laws of divorce. The procedure of divorce was indeed complex, requiring expert knowledge and experience. This helped to guard against a hasty termination of a human and sacred relationship. An effective safeguard against precipitate divorce was also the obligation of the husband to pay his spouse, on divorce, the marriage settlement, the *Ketubah*.[22]

The Rabbis fixed a minimum amount for the marriage settlement which could not be reduced, namely, two hundred *zuz* in the case of the marriage of a virgin and one hundred *zuz* in the case of a widow or divorcee. Because of their regard for those who have lost their natural provider and protector they adhered rigidly to this regulation. The minimum amount of the marriage settlement could be and often was increased generously. Indeed, the Rabbis recommended, notwithstanding an opposing view,[23] an increase in the marriage settlement.[24] The rules relating to payment of the settlement also applied in many respects to the "increase".[25]

There were further provisions made which were clearly designed to protect the financial position of the divorced woman. The payment of the marriage settlement to the wife was not only a protection for her but, it may be suggested, also for the husband who might otherwise be led to disrupt hastily his matrimonial relationship.

It is often assumed that in Jewish law the husband can divorce his wife against her will. This mistaken idea is based on a literal reading of the words of the Torah,[26]

22 Ketuboth 10b
23 Ibid.
24 Ketuboth 54b
25 S.A.E.H. 93 and 94
26 Deuteronomy 24,1

"and he can send her away". Jewish law would not allow the husband such freedom of divorce. The prohibition, referred to above, against the re-marriage with his wife who had become the wife of another man who had since divorced her or died, was certainly a restriction that might prevent hasty divorce. Indeed, the duty devolved upon the Rabbis to bring about reconciliation.

The ordinances of Rabbenu Gershom, which prohibit polygamy and insist on the consent of husband and wife to a divorce among Ashkenazic Jews, still hold sway. They helped to equalize the rights of husband and wife in marriage and divorce law.[27] The legislation of the Rabbis of the Talmud and the enactments they promulgated, served Rabbenu Gershom as a basis and example. Behind halachic legislation was the inalienable right of every human being to independence and freedom. Under all circumstances the husband and wife could preserve their individuality. The concept of marriage as subjugation of the wife to the husband, both in person and property, was repugnant to the Sages.

Many rules in the Talmud and Codes testify to the consideration that was to be accorded to a divorced wife.[28] In terminating what was intended to be a permanent relationship the husband was to show regard and practical sympathy and to offer financial help to his divorced wife.

Divorce is among the most perplexing social problems of our times. The number of broken marriages is large and rising. The break-down of a marriage is always beset with sadness and frustration. It calls for both censure and sympathy. All marriages are subject to pressures and

27   S.A.E.H. 1,9-10; Ḥatam Sofer E.H,2
28   S.A.E.H. 100,1; 119,8 Rema; S.A.E.H. 66,10: עולה עמו ואינה יורדת עמו

emotions. Parties have different backgrounds, attitudes and interests and while in the majority of cases love and affection combine with character and understanding to mould and foster a happy relationship many couples in modern times are impatient and hasty. The strain and tension that inevitably follow are too much for them to bear. A period of adjustment, counselling and guidance, discussion and advice are sometimes of help in avoiding the final and regrettable break. Whenever efforts have failed and divorce is unavoidable couples need sympathy, support and encouragement.

The legal definition of מוררת, a rebellious wife, is difficult and complex.[29] It has reference to a wife who denies the husband his conjugal rights. It also connotes a wife who refuses to work thus depriving the husband of her earnings. If a woman refuses to live with her husband without offering a reasonable ground, she can be divorced and she forfeits her right to the *Ketubah*. She is, however, entitled to the property she brought with her. This view, it would seem, gained recognition in Jewish communities in Germany. It has been suggested that many Jewish women at that time participated in the economic life of the country. While some were happy to support their husbands who devoted themselves piously to study, others having gained economic independence desired greater liberation and freedom. Hence we find a larger number of cases of intractable wives.

R. Hayyim Or Zarua, a disciple of R. Meir of Rothenburg, writes in one of his responsa[30] that, "when the number of women who deserted their husbands had increased, R. Meir wrote to R. Yedidia who was at the

---

29 Ketuboth 63a
30 R. Hayyim Or Zarua 69,126,191

time Rabbi of Speyer and the adjacent communities, to meet him in order to ordain that a wife deserting her husband should lose her rights in respect of the *Ketubah.* She should also forfeit whatever property she brought to her husband". This is clearly a reference to a sort of synod convoked under R. Meir. It is evidence of a serious situation that had arisen in his day. The position demanded urgent action. R. Meir writes: "The Communities ordained when they were assembled at Nuremberg that in any case where a woman leaves her husband, influenced by her relatives, the husband can divorce her against her will and retain all her property if she fails to return to him after being warned to do so by the court. It is proper that all Israel shall obey this *Takkanah*".[31] He adds, "Since there is no fear that she will be driven from the Jewish fold, as there is no Gentile involved, the law ought to be placed on its Biblical level that a wife's possessions are the property of her husband."

This stringent ordinance adopted by the communities must have been prompted by the desertions of many women. Because of their lax religious and moral standards they came under the category of "rebellious wives".[32] The *Takkanah,* founded on Talmudic law, was clearly designed to protect the husband against the "rebellious wife."[33] She would forfeit her marriage settlement when divorced.[34] A wife that transgresses the law of Moses was among those who could have their marriage dissolved without receiving what was due to

---

31 Hagahot Maimuni, Ishuth 14,13
32 Hagahot Asheri Kiddushin, 191
33 M. Ketuboth 7,6
34 Ketuboth 63a-b

them. Other problems confronting the family find full
and vivid expression in the rabbinic sources.

The Rabbis praise the husband who loves his wife as
himself and honours her more than himself. They
promise him domestic peace and happiness.[35]

Rab warned husbands to be most careful not to hurt
their wives since their tears are frequent and they are
quickly hurt. "Since the destruction of the Temple,"
another Sage declared, "the gates of prayer are locked
but not the gates of tears".[36] Because their tears well from
the depth of the heart God hears their petition.

Generally speaking Jewish husbands were generous to
their wives and their conduct was in harmony with
rabbinic teaching. While felicitous relations prevailed
among most couples there were cases, as the sources
testify, of ill-treatment of wives. Where a husband
resorted to assault upon his wife he was severely
reprimanded by the court. Isserls writes: "A husband
who, without the wife's provocation, beats her is deemed
a transgressor. If he does so habitually the court must
place him under a ban and make him undertake solemnly
that he will cease to resort to violence. If he does not obey
the order of the court some authorities hold that after one
or two warnings he can be coerced to divorce. A Jew is
always to respect and honour his wife and even if she is a
shrew he must not assault her".[37]

Some rabbinic authorities ruled that a husband who
ill-treats his wife must provide her with separate
maintenance like the "one who had gone overseas".[38] In a

35 Sanhedrin 76b
36 Baba Metzia 59a
37 S.A.E.H. 154,3
38 Ibid 70,5

case of continuing ill-treatment she could live away from him but he would nevertheless be compelled to support her. This would indicate that the Halachah recognised 'judicial separation' without divorce. In certain cases the offending husband was compelled to add to the marriage settlement according to his financial position.[39] That guilty husbands were to be dealt with harshly by the communities was to prevent a rare practice becoming widespread.

Other family difficulties are dealt with in the Halachah. Maimonides[40] ruled that the husband and wife have a right to prevent certain members of their respective families visiting the matrimonial home. While the husband need give no reason for his objection to the wife's relatives visiting his home, in the case of the wife she had to give a valid reason for her refusal to allow the husband's parents and other relations to visit the matrimonial abode. If they cause her aggravation and distress she can refuse to allow them to visit the home. Revealingly, in the case of the husband, Maimonides mentions the following relatives of the wife: parents, brothers, sisters, but in the case of the wife, her objection appears to be limited to the husband's mother and sisters.[41] Whether or not the wife has to prove that she is being aggravated and distressed or her statement is sufficient to veto the husband's relatives' visits is not clear from the text. It would seem that the husband's rights in this matter exceed those of the wife.

The home, according to one authority, belongs to the husband and not to the wife. Hers is a right of

---

39   Maimonides: Ishuth 14,15; S.A.E.H. 76,1
40   Maimonides: Ishuth 13,14
41   Yebamoth 117a; S.A.E.H. 17,4; Ibid 74,10

accommodation and use but not of ownership.[42] Maimonides' ruling does not necessarily concede ownership of the husband בעלות but rather rests on consideration of human nature. The intrusion of certain relatives might affect domestic peace and harmony. The *Tur* is of the opinion that Maimonides ruled that both parties have equal rights. In recent years English law has held that each party has an equal share in the matrimonial home.

Jewish law shows special concern for the widow and seeks to compensate her for the loss of her natural protector.[43] The Rabbis ruled that the court was to give precedence to the complainant widow in a case, immediately after that of orphans.[44] The financial position of the widow was to be firmly protected. While a wife does not inherit her husband, by rabbinic extension of the law, he inherits his wife and he takes precedence over all other heirs. With property in which the deceased had only expectancy, all heirs, including the firstborn son, take equally.

In the event of the husband's death the marriage settlement and the additional increase were to be paid to the widow; the property the wife brought before marriage for which the husband assumed responsibility was to be returned to her. The property which the wife brought before marriage for which the husband did not assume responsibility was to be returned to the widow together with any improvement effected. The rules referred to were designed for the welfare of the widow.

As long as the widow did not remarry her maintenance

42 Maggid Mishneh, Ishuth 13,14
43 Maimonides: De'oth vi. 10
44 S.A.Ḥ.M 15,2

had to be paid. She enjoyed priority of payment over the maintenance of minor daughters and over the dowry of older daughters. For her maintenance was thus the first charge on the deceased husband's estate. Her entitlement took precedence over gifts or charitable donations bequeathed by the husband. The widow's provision included accommodation, clothes and fees for medical services.[45]

The institution of levirate marriage יבום[46] reflects the cohesion and importance of the family in Judaism. In Latin *levir* means a husband's brother, a brother-in-law. Levirate marriage has reference to the marriage with the widow of a brother who died without offspring. Through such a marriage the family line would not become extinct, the name of the deceased brother might be continued and his property would remain in the family. Where such a marriage was not desired, the woman could be freed to marry another man by the procedure of *Halitzah,* a procedure which dissolved the bond between the childless widow and the brother-in-law. However, from Talmudic times[47] as levirate marriage was not always regarded by the parties as a *mitzvah* of the Torah, *Halitzah* and not *Yibum* has been practised almost universally.

The question of the *agunah* — the woman who does not know the whereabouts of her husband or whether he is alive or not — has been the subject of considerable controversy in modern times. While there is no presumption of death in Jewish law, the attitude of the

45 Ketuboth 52b; Maimonides: Ishuth 18,1-5; S.A.E.H. 93-94,1 and Rema
46 Deuteronomy 25,5-10
47 Yebamoth 3a;39b

Rabbis to this question manifests leniency.[48] The
problem exercised their minds and they showed great
sympathy and consideration. They relaxed the laws of
evidence in regard to the *agunah*. Thus the evidence of a
woman was accepted. So was the testimony of a
disinterested Gentile. To prevent a wife becoming an
agunah the Sages showed unusual leniency in some of the
otherwise strict rules which surrounded the גט, the bill of
divorcement. While normally the testimony of two
witnesses were required in Jewish law yet the שליח, the
agent duly appointed by the husband to deliver the *get,*
was permitted to testify alone.[49] Again, in the matter of
the witnesses to the *get* the Sages showed the same
attitude.[50] Maimonides expresses similar concern and
consideration.[51] A phrase used by the Rabbis reflects
their deep concern and compassion for women "so that
the daughters of Israel shall not remain tied to their
absent husbands."[52]

It is significant that in the case of an *agunah* evidence
based on recognition of the voice of the husband was also
accepted.[53] The evidence of one witness who had heard
from another was equally admissible.[54] The lenient
attitude was founded on the firm belief that a woman
would not wish to remarry unless convinced by evidence
that her husband had died.[55] In the case of an *agunah*,
provided the evidence given was certain and definite, the

---

48   Ibid. 87a;88a
49   Gittin 2b-3a
50   Ibid. 26a
51   Gerushin 1,23
52   Ibid. כדי שלא יהיו בנות ישראל עגונות
53   Gittin 3a
54   Yebamoth 88a
55   Ibid. 87b

court was advised to accept it and permit the woman to remarry.[56]

The solicitude of the Rabbis for the general welfare of women may be seen from a case recorded in the Talmud.[57] The famous sage R. Tarfon was of priestly lineage and possessed of considerable wealth. In a time of famine he betrothed three hundred women so that they might exercise their right as the wives of a Priest in sharing or buying *terumah* which only priests, their wives and children were permitted to eat. According to the strict law the daughter of an Israelite who became betrothed to a priest was allowed to eat *terumah,* but the Rabbis forbade it as a defensive measure; as she remained in her father's home until her נשואין she might share the *terumah* with her brothers and sisters. While it had been suggested that the figure of 300 may stand for a round number, R. Tarfon no doubt based his action upon the legal notion of marriage, a notion which does not distinguish between marriage in the accepted sense and a legal marriage which equally binds the parties who have become betrothed, in order to bestow the priestly status

56 After the Holocaust acknowledged rabbinic authorities were called upon to deal with the vexed problem that faced large numbers of women whose husbands could not be traced. The Rabbanut Harashit of Israel set up a special Beth Din to deal with such cases. Chief Rabbi I. Herzog, in consultation with Rabbi S.D. Kahana, the famous Rav of the Old City, formerly of the Warsaw Rabbinate, found it possible to permit many such widows to remarry. During the same period the London Beth Din was similarly preoccupied with many cases of *Agunah.* Large numbers were permitted to remarry in accordance with the Halachah. See Rabbi I.J. Weiss, Responsa: Minḥath Yitzḥak. Vol. I,1-5.

57 J. Yebamoth 4,12; Tosefta Ketuboth 5,1; *terumah* could doubtless be bought cheaply as the number of potential consumers was limited. It has been suggested that R. Tarfon's action may have been motivated by his desire to protect these women against the attentions of Roman soldiers.

upon the priest's spouse. His action was clearly intended to help the impoverished women.

That R. Tarfon had a deep concern for the poor is evident from another incident which testifies to the humanity of this jurist. He was indeed a worthy representative of those who always supported the woman's cause. It is related of him that whilst he was teaching his disciples, a bride passed before him (in all likelihood she was of the poorer classes and possibly an orphan). He ordered that she should be brought into his home. He then asked his wife and his mother to bathe her, anoint her, adorn her and dance with her until she went to the husband's house.[58]

The Mishnah[59] reflects the Rabbis' sensitive respect for the personal feelings of women. Indeed, they ruled that such feelings were a ground for divorce. "And these are the persons whom the court can force to divorce their wives; he that is afflicted with boils, or that has a polypus or that collects dog's excrements or that is a coppersmith or a tanner, whether these defects were in them before they married or whether they arose after they were married." The fact that even if the woman knew of the defects before she could claim that she thought that she could adjust to such defects but found herself unable to endure them.

In the foregoing pages I quoted examples which testify to the Rabbis' recognition of the high status of women. Critics, however, have persistently pointed to the benediction in the Morning Service in which a Jewish male gives thanks to God for not having been born a

---

58 Aboth D'Rabbi Nathan ch. 41,13, Soncino edition
59 Ketuboth 7,10

woman.[60] The blessing is taken from the Talmud[61] and it has reference to the privilege that men have in fulfilling many precepts which do not devolve upon women.[62] But many other vital tasks in the Jewish scheme of living which women perform with zeal and enthusiasm are no less important for the cohesion and continuance of Judaism.

The Jewish wife and mother has always enjoyed love and affection, respect and reverence. One principle enunciated in the Halachah bears testimony, stronger than social convention or chivalry, to the high status accorded her by the Sages. They expressed it succinctly and with emotion: "The woman rises to a higher level in marriage; but she does not go down to a lower level with the husband".[63]

While there was a seeming lower status of a woman in law, in life her position ranked high. Indeed, the Sages were deeply concerned about her dignity and honour quoting the words of the Psalmist:[64] "The honour of a princess is within the palace." Her dignity and honour did not free her from communal or national duties. In the case of a "mandatory war" women were obliged to serve provisions for the army.[65]

That the religious obligations devolving upon men and women in Judaism vary is due rather to their respective responsibilities than to the relegation of women, as is sometimes asserted, to a subordinate position. Similarly,

60 Authorized Prayer Book p.62
61 Menahoth 43b
62 Abudraham: Morning Service; Tur O.H. 46
63 Ketuboth 48a; Adret VII, 57
64 Psalm 45, 14
65 M. Sotah 8,7 See Tiferet Yisrael ad loc. and R. Samuel Strashun, Annotations on M. Sotah 8,7

the segregation of the sexes in the Synagogue and the House of Study is based on the teaching of modesty and the need for devotion in prayer stressed in Jewish teaching.[66]

While women are exempt from the performance of such positive precepts as are bound by time מצות עשה שהזמן גרמא Rabbenu Tam[67] ruled that they are permitted to perform these *mitzvoth* and to pronounce the appropriate blessings. The principle of "a blessing in vain" did not apply. The Ashkenazi communities have followed the decision of Rabbenu Tam. Among the Sephardi authorities there is a division of opinion.[68]

The Talmudic ruling which permits a partner in a courtyard to object to some activities by the other partners in the courtyard does not apply to women who do their washing there. The reason given by the Rabbis is "on account of the honour due to the daughters of Israel". While this exemption was clearly prompted by moral considerations of privacy and propriety to be observed by women, it equally testifies to the high personal status of women in Jewish law.[69]

Among the ten enactments ordained by Ezra was the one that permitted pedlars to travel about in the town selling spicery and perfumes for women even against the wishes of the townspeople.[70]

The disqualification of women as witnesses appears

66 Sukkah 51b
67 Rosh, Kiddushin, 1,49
68 S.A.O.Ḥ. 589,6
69 J. Baba Bathra 1,5; J. Nedarim 5,1
70 Baba Kamma 82a; Baba Bathra 22a. On the enactments of Ezra see Hoffmann Magazin 1883, 48ff. The Talmud says that pedlars were allowed to sell spicery and jewelry so that women should remain attractive to their husbands.

to stand in sharp contrast to the status and respect accorded them in Jewish law. In certain cases the evidence of a woman is accepted. As already said regarding an *agunah* a woman's testimony is admitted. Similarly, in the case of a wife suspected of infidelity the evidence of a woman is accepted.[71] Concerning the rite to be performed for an untraced murder if a woman says that she had seen the murderer she is believed and no heifer-rite was necessary.[72] If a captive woman says that she was not defiled her testimony is admissible and she is permitted to marry a Cohen.[73] In regard to a girl's age in the case of *Halitzah,* a woman's evidence is accepted.[74] Where one witness is sufficient in Jewish law the testimony of a woman is likewise valid.

Two reasons have been suggested why women are generally disqualified as witnesses. The disqualification is not because of their incredibility or inferior status. Nor are they suspected of giving false testimony.[75] Two witnesses were required to give evidence before the court and such witnesses were subjected to searching questioning. The honour and dignity due to women, who are shy and modest by nature, are incompatible with attendance at court and its regime. Submission of women to cross-examination, whether in capital or other cases, would hardly be consistent with their dignity and

71 Sotah 47a-b
72 Ibid.
73 Ketuboth 27a
74 Niddah 48b; S.A.E.H. 155,15
75 Responsa: Mishpete Uziel H.M. 20. Chief Rabbi Uziel suggests that as women are generally not engaged in business or financial matters they are not used to paying meticulous attention to what they have witnessed. They may easily err in recalling incidents or events. But in all matters in which they have experience and about which they are particular we rely on their evidence.

sensitivity. Although in monetary cases the law abolished "searching questioning" it insisted on clarification.[76] This was a legal procedural requirement which would still necessitate their appearance at court.[77] A communal enactment could, however, permit the evidence of women to be accepted in monetary cases, but not in cases of personal status, e.g. marriage and divorce.[78]

A psychological reason has also been suggested for the disqualification of women as witnesses. Being by nature more emotional and imaginative[79] their evidence may not always be entirely objective.[80] Testimony must be based on close observation of facts.

Nowhere is the concern for the integrity of the family more strongly reflected than in the Jewish law of inheritance. The Torah lays down a definitive order of succession. To this order the Rabbis added other members of the family and their descendants, as well as the husband. Indeed, members of the family only had a vested right to inheritance.[81] For the law of inheritance rests on blood kinship.

The Torah emphasizes: "And it shall be unto the children of Israel a statute of judgment".[82] Hence this law was not subject to change and any stipulation qualifying it was not valid. Whether the deceased gave instructions concerning disinheritance when he was in health or while he was lying sick they had no validity. The rules and regulations relating to inheritance reflect a high moral

76   S.A.H.M. 30,61
77   Gittin 41a
78   S.A.H.M. 35,14 Rema; Responsa: Mishpete Uziel H.M. 20
79   Yebamoth 113b; 114a
80   Ibid. 118a Tosafoth
81   Numbers 27,1-11; Baba Bathra 115a ff; S.A.H.M. 276
82   Numbers 27,11

concept. But whilst Jewish law limited the testator's rights in so far as he had to adhere to the natural degree of relationship, he could bequeath gifts to whom he desired. It is only when he indicated his wish in the language of inheritance that it was of no effect. If, however, his instructions were in the general form of a gift they were valid.[83] Indeed, the heirs had a solemn duty to carry out the words of the deceased. Yet, morally he was restricted. Maimonides states: "He who gives away his property to a stranger, leaving out his heirs, incurs the displeasure of the Sages. Even if his heirs did not treat him well his action would be frowned upon. Legally, however, the donees would acquire the title to all the property left to them".[84]

Modern jurists advocate the need to limit the freedom of testation and English law has moved in recent times towards this attitude.[85]

Moral and humane imperatives clearly underlie the Jewish laws of inheritance. These laws helped materially to maintain the integrity and cohesion of the family.

That a wife according to Biblical and rabbinic law[86] does not inherit her husband is not in conflict with the view that the laws of inheritance have served to strengthen the bonds of family unity. It was perhaps thought unfair that in the event of the widow remarrying, the first husband's estate would not remain in his family. If the second husband and his family were to be in possession of the first husband's property this could lead to strife and tension in the domestic relationship.

83   Maimonides: Inheritance 6,5
84   Gittin 15a; Inheritance 6,11
85   Rabbi K. Kahana-Kagan, "Three Great Systems of Jurisprudence" pp 76,152 note 99
86   Baba Bathra 111b

But Jewish law made adequate provision for the widow's benefit. She was entitled to her *Ketubah,* marriage settlement[87] and the dowry she had brought to her husband. A wife's property was divided, according to Talmudic legislation, into two categories. One was known as "the property of iron sheep" and has reference to the property which she brought with her as a dowry. Such property would be mentioned in the *Ketubah* and for this property the husband assumed responsibility. The somewhat strange name נכסי צאן ברזל can be explained as property indestructible as iron. The profit accruing to the husband from such property is as certain as the wool that sheep grow. The second is described as נכסי מלוג "the property of plucking" and relates to property acquired by the wife subsequently to the betrothal, from which the husband "plucked" the fruit without being responsible for loss of capital or deterioration.[88] As already mentioned Talmudical and post-Talmudical enactments laid down rules for the widow's maintenance which took precedence over the inheritance of the heirs as well as over gifts made by the deceased.[89]

The position of daughters in the law of inheritance is seen by critics as evidence of the inferior status accorded to women. An echo of Sadducean criticism is found in the Talmud.[90] But basic to inheritance is an entirely different concept. It is a natural desire of a father that his son should succeed him. This desire is perhaps motivated by, at least, two considerations; that the name should be continued and the estate should remain in the family.

87 Numbers 27,8-11; Baba Bathra 113ff; S.A.Ḥ.M 276-290
88 Nedarim 88a ;Adret 2,390,395
89 Baba Bathra 140b; Maimonides: Ishuth 18,1-5
90 J. Baba Bathra 8,1; Shabbath 116b.

Hence where there is no son the deceased's brother inherits.[91]

The position of daughters, however, is safeguarded in Jewish law. The Sages made due provision for their support. They are to be maintained from the father's estate until marriage and to be given a dowry.[92] Where the estate is large the sons inherit in the normal way but the daughters have to be provided for first.[93] If it is small, the daughters receive maintenance and the sons do not inherit. The obligation to provide for the daughters' needs devolved upon the male heirs. The dowries for daughters were to be according to the social standing and material possessions of the father. If a father on his deathbed stipulated that his daughters should not be maintained out of his estate, his instructions are to be ignored and all needs provided for them.[94]

The firstborn male, unless posthumous, takes a double share in the father's estate.[95] He is obliged to defray a double share of the outstanding debts owed by his deceased father.[96] The firstborn is entitled, even if he is illegitimate, to a double portion and is obliged to meet a double share of the father's debts. A firstborn among daughters, who inherits in the absence of sons, does not enjoy the right of a firstborn male. Regarding step-children some husbands took upon themselves the obligation to maintain these who became part of their family after marriage with the mother. Such maintenance

---

91 Baba Bathra 110b and Tosafoth
92 M. Ketuboth 4,6; 13,3; 9,1
93 Baba Bathra 139b, 140a
94 Ketuboth 70a
95 Baba Bathra 122b. A first born received a double share of the available assets but not of what was to come in later into the estate.
96 Ibid. 124a

was to be provided at the family board. A step-daughter could not claim money in lieu of maintenance.[97] That children and relatives born out of wedlock or of an invalid marriage of the deceased are his kin and legal heirs rests on the principle of kinship.[98]

The parent-child relationship in Jewish law has its own characteristics. It is based on the commandment which enjoins the duty to honour parents. Parents, particularly fathers, have legal rights over daughters while they are minors. These rights were intended for the welfare of the children and for their protection against abuses. It was, however, the opinion of the Sages that once a daughter becomes a *'bogeret',* that is reaches the age of twelve years and six months, parents have no longer legal authority over her.[99] It was thought that at that age daughters have minds of their own and must be given responsibility for their own actions. To allow anyone, even parents, to have legal rights over them would imply a lack of acknowledgment of their individuality. Yet the recognition of children's independence and status, far from affecting the cohesion of the family, has helped to sustain it and enhance family bonds and sanctities.

Many problems that plagued the ancient world in regard to family matters rarely confronted the Jewish community. Whence did the strength of the Jewish family stem? From the religious obligations that devolved upon parents. The duty of the father to teach his children the laws of the Torah,[100] and the constant awareness that under the higher laws, "the laws of heaven", the father, as

97   S.A.E.H. 114,1
98   Yebamoth 2,5; S.A.Ḥ.M. 276,6
99   Ketuboth 39a; Rashi ad loc
100 Deuteronomy 11,19-21 and Sifre Deuteronomy 46

head of the family, was fully responsible for the action of his children,[101] could not but strengthen family loyalties. In rabbinic thought the duty of honouring parents is equivalent to the duty of honouring God.[102] This emphasized that children, regardless of their age, owed obedience to their parents whenever such obedience did not conflict with the moral and religious imperatives which devolved upon every Jew.[103]

While a duty lies upon children to provide parents in need with food, drink and other necessities it is not a legal obligation. It is included among the religious and moral duties. In Judaism, love of children for parents combined with strong family ties, rendered special legal provisions superfluous. In the opinion of the Rabbis the honour due to parents as enjoined in the Ten Commandments is an absolute obligation. It is not children's reward to parents for past efforts on their behalf in childhood or youth. It rests on feelings of love and affection. In the view of the Rabbis, with those commandments the reward for which is stated in the Torah, the courts need not concern themselves.[104] The commentators in explaining this view suggest that family links and natural respect of children for parents were a guarantee that children would maintain parents in need.[105]

Equally, deep parental love and care for the wellbeing of their children made legal rulings unnecessary. They would care for their children with tenderness without the intrusion of the law.[106] A saying attributed to the scholars

101 Yebamoth 62b
102 J. Peah 1,1
103 Kiddushin 32a
104 Hullin 11b
105 Kiddushin 31a-b
106 Ketuboth 49a

of Usha declares that he who maintains his young sons and daughters is performing a righteous act.[107] A fundamental principle in Jewish law in regard to children's needs is to be stressed. All members of the family enjoy personal freedom. Even minors are not subject to the legal authority of their parents. They are entitled to acquire and sell for themselves movable property over which parents have no legal rights.[108]

From the law of the rebellious son[109] it is clear that both father and mother had to testify against him. Theirs was a joint authority. His punishment, however, had to be decided by the court and not by the parents.

Other rules of right conduct generated love and loyalty. Parents were not allowed to show favouritism to one of their children.[110] Such an attitude, the Rabbis urged, would cause quarrels and dissension in the family.[111] A father was obliged to provide a home on marriage for his eldest son first.[112] He was not permitted to disinherit a wicked son in favour of a good son.[113] Indeed, the Sages, as already mentioned, strongly disapproved of disinheriting children.[114] While children owe honour and respect to parents, the latter were not to impose burdens upon them.[115] It is proper for parents to maintain children up to the age of thirteen.[116] According to the Rabbis a father owed five main duties to his sons.

107   Ibid. 49b
108   M. Gittin 5,7 and Gittin 59a; Maimonides: Mechirah 29,6
109   Deuteronomy 21,18ff
110   Shabbath 10b
111   Ibid.
112   Sotah 34b
113   Baba Bathra 133b
114   Ibid.
115   Maimonides: Mamrim 6,8
116   Ketuboth 49b; Genesis Rabbah 63,14

He must circumcise them, redeem them, teach them Torah; he must also teach them a trade and help them to marry. Another opinion adds — to teach them to swim.[117]

If a father has become mentally affected the court is obliged to administer his estate providing out of it for his sons and daughters.[118] In the relationship of parents and children reciprocal duties are enjoined. Thus a son should be coerced to maintain his father, to provide for him board and clothes and generally to look after his welfare.[119] Even if the son lives on charity it is his duty to honour and help his parents. The Rabbis ruled that a proselyte must not maltreat, curse or shame his non-Jewish father. Children must honour parents in life and death.[120]

Central to the relationship of parents and children were the doctrines of the sacredness of human personality and of individual accountability. Every human being has a mind of his own and is responsible for his actions. In Jewish law no one can become the possession or chattel of another.[121]

Adoption in Jewish law differs fundamentally from that in other legal systems and legislation. The essence of the family, as we noted, rests on blood kinship. Accordingly, the Halachah does not regard adoption as a legal institution. In Judaism, adoption is considered a benevolent act, a charitable and worthy deed, creating a form of parental guardianship.[122] A deep love of

117   J. Kiddushin 1,7; Kiddushin 29a; Tosefta Kiddushin 1,8
118   Ketuboth 48a
119   Kiddushin 31a-b
120   Semahoth 9,19
121   Berakoth 17a
122   Sanhedrin 19b

children and devotion to home life have moved many a childless Jewish couple to realize their ideal and cherished longing through adoption. But the adopted child, loved and affectionately cared for by the adoptive family, remains in status the offspring of its natural parents. In Jewish law the adoptive parents have obligations to the adopted child.[123] They assume responsibility for his physical and mental welfare and his financial position, including maintenance and matters of inheritance.[124]

In Judaism the education of children was considered of first importance. The Biblical injunction to teach the children the words of the Torah[125] was amplified and emphasized by the Sages.[126] Education was so important that parents were permitted to make the necessary arrangements and negotiate terms and fees with a teacher even on the Sabbath.[127] The teaching of a trade, as has been mentioned, was also considered a duty devolving upon parents. Lack of a trade may lead the young to delinquency.[128] Parents were similarly allowed to discuss the proposed betrothal of their children on the Sabbath.[129] Like education the marriage of their children was a duty of parents.[130]

Reverence for old age is one of the most admirable characteristics of the human race. Individuals and nations regard old age with awe and love. The Torah

123   Maimonides: Ishuth 23,17-18
124   Ketuboth 101b; S.A.E.H. 114,7; S.A.H.M. 60,2-5
125   Deuteronomy 6,7
126   Kiddushin 29a-b and 30a
127   Shabbath 150a
128   Kiddushin 30b
129   Shabbath 150a
130   Kiddushin 29a

enjoins respect, reverence and honour for the old.[131] The most meticulous care and attention must be bestowed upon them. The treatment of the aged must not be dictated by social or selfish considerations but it must be by an inner and higher motivation. The attitude of the Halachah to the old reflects the same lofty concept.

Before concluding this survey of family law, a few crucial problems affecting many a Jewish domestic scene prompt comment.

The problem of the *mamzer*[132] is most painful and distressing. Defined as a child born of an adulterous or incestuous relationship the *mamzer* (bastard) and *mamzeret* (female bastard) are forbidden to marry a Jew of legitimate birth. Whilst allowed to marry persons of similar birth and status, or converts to Judaism, the children of such a union will sadly have the same status as the illegitimate parent. Hence such marriages are generally discouraged. The fear of *mamzerut* would make the free intermarriage among Jews, in different communities, very difficult.

The reason for the Biblical precept is clear. Maimonides has summed it up solemnly. He writes: "In order to create a horror of illicit relationships a *mamzer* was not allowed to marry an Israelite woman. The adulterer and adulteress were thus taught that by their action they bring upon their offspring irreparable injury."[133] Their children's status and attendant plight might serve as a stern warning to would-be guilty parents.

Where Jewish life was strong *mamzerut* was extremely rare. In modern times, the increased incidence of *mamzerut* has exercised the minds of contemporary

131   Leviticus 19,32
132   Deuteronomy 23,3
133   Guide III,49

halachic authorities, all the more, as in all other respects, religious, spiritual and in inheritance, the *mamzer* enjoys the rights and privileges of a Jew.

Orthodox rabbinates have always dealt with each individual case with very deep concern and profound sympathy. They applied their knowledge, experience and understanding, paying the most scrupulous attention to all the evidence, in an earnest endeavour to arrive, wherever possible, at a favourable decision within the sanction of the Halachah.

The Sages of the Midrash gave touching expression to their humane feeling and profound sympathy for the illegitimate when they applied to them the words of Ecclesiastes:[134] "But I returned and considered all the oppression that goes on under the sun: the tears of the oppressed with none to comfort them; and on the side of their oppressors there was power — with none to comfort them".

Daniel the Tailor,[135] in a bold homily, echoes what was clearly poignant criticism of the harsh law. The homily deserves to be quoted in full because it is marked by pathos and unusual daring. It runs thus: "Daniel the Tailor explained the verse as referring to children of forbidden relationships. 'Behold the tears of the oppressed' — their parents sinned, but what has that to do with these unfortunate ones? The father has sinned in giving him birth but how has the son sinned? On the side of their oppressor there was power, the power of the Torah, as administered by the Great Sanhedrin, who restrained them from marrying into the Congregation. 'With none to comfort them', God says, 'It is for me to

134   4,1
135   Leviticus Rabbah 32,7; Koheleth Rabbah 4,3

comfort them because in this life they are impure but in the future world they will be like the 'candlestick of God' which the Prophet Zechariah saw in his vision'."

Few Midrashic gleanings are replete with a deeper concern and humanity for the fate of the deprived and despondent. The law could not be changed because it would undermine the integrity and sanctity of the family. But the Divine assurance regarding the future would give some solace and strength to the innocent children and wipe away their sorrowful tears.

Intermarriage is another crucial problem in present-day Jewish life. It is, alas, widespread and formidable. In Western Europe and in the United States it has assumed proportions which cause Jewish leadership the gravest anxiety. The issue is all the more serious because it is not confined to one particular class. It is found in almost all sections of the community, intellectual and non-intellectual, poor and prosperous, the humblest and the highest. A cloud of darkness and anguish hangs over many Jewish homes and families.

Now intermarriage leads directly to the subject of proselytisation. The halachic demands are known. Battei Din are often subjected to considerable criticism for a rigid and uncompromising attitude. The critics fail to realize how difficult it is for one born and nurtured in another faith to assume the duties of Jewish observance and to integrate himself or herself as a practising and loyal member of a community with its own religious way of life.

An applicant for proselytisation is required to show evidence of sincerity and belief in the fundamental principles of Judaism. He is also to have, at least, a rudimentary knowledge of Jewish religious practice. In the case of marriage it is logical and reasonable to insist that the Jewish partner show an example of Jewish religious observance in daily life. Indeed, in many cases it is necessary for the Jewish spouse to undergo a kind of spiritual conversion and change of his or her life-style. Persons who manifest sincerity and willingness to live in accordance with these requirements are accorded sympathy, consideration and encouragement during the period of preparation for conversion to Judaism. Orthodox rabbinates deal with such aspirants with human insight and compassion and finally admit them to Judaism according to the Halachah.

In Judaism, which is a living faith, the question of family purity and morality is sacred and fundamental. The Torah, the Talmud and the Codes devote a great deal of detailed attention to the laws of טהרת המשפחה which, in tender and cherished privacy, regulate marital life. These laws have helped to foster in Jewish home-life a spirit of modesty and refinement and to enhance the personal relations between the sexes.

Underlying these laws is the doctrine of the dignity of the individual and the sanctity of the family. They have contributed to moral conduct, self-restraint and domestic peace and happiness. They have served as a powerful bond between husband and wife, a bond sustained by impeccable fidelity and strengthened by regular spiritual renewal. A closer study of these regulations is not within the compass of this work. But a deeper appreciation of their significance and humanity would assuredly help to lessen the marital stress and strain of many Jewish couples and lead to a reduction in marriage failures. Indeed, a perceptive understanding of the sanctities and ethical values of the very institution of marriage would serve to restore the Jewish family to our great and sacred heritage.

The principles and doctrines of religion, the law and morals, discussed in this chapter, are relevant to contemporary social reality. The unity and integrity of the family have been widely assailed in the past decades. It is one of the major maladies of modern times. Radical changes in moral standards and modes of behaviour have resulted in rapidly increasing infidelities, in single-parent families, and in a formidable incidence of deliquency and crime. While other factors, too, account for the present situation, the absence of a religious background and a lack of parental responsibility in many homes have clearly contributed materially to the current trends. A return to religious values embracing every sphere of human experience would help to restore to the family its former influence, strength and stability.

CHAPTER FIVE

THE INDIVIDUAL AND THE COMMUNITY

The Mishnah[1] casts a rich light on the attitude to the individual. The Rabbis speak of his unique position and his worth for posterity. "Man", they declare, "was created single, as an individual". And he was created in the Divine image. Hence the sanctity and dignity of every human being.

The Sages stressed the nature and character of the Divine creation by the simple illustration of God who stamps every individual with the seal of the first man, yet not one of them is like his fellow. "Therefore", the Mishnah continues, "every man must say 'For my sake the world was created'." The meaning is clear and compelling. It emphasizes the grave responsibility that rests upon every individual. If one says 'for my sake the world was created' he thereby acknowledges that he must be held to account for his actions. He cannot free himself from the obligations which his supreme status imposes upon him. The concepts of morality and humanity flow from man's primacy. Vast opportunities are open to the individual. But his very supremacy demands high standards of conduct, humility and integrity.

1 Sanhedrin 4,5

Yet brotherhood and fellowship are implicit in Jewish teaching.[2] The Mishnah[3] enumerates a number of religious rites, the public performance of which requires a minimum of ten males. Accordingly, ten adults, the number that constitutes a congregation, are necessary for Divine Service. God is sanctified in the midst of the congregation. Significantly, our very prayers are in the plural expressing the sentiment of the house of Israel. The individual gains spiritually from his personal association with the community. Indeed, a familiar rabbinic dictum warns against separating oneself from the community.[4]

The concept of corporate responsibility and mutual aid is central to Jewish teaching and the organized community makes it easier for its members to fulfil their religious rites and educational needs.

The Rabbis were concerned about the preservation of the freedom and the respective rights of the individual and the community. As may be seen from the sources, they zealously guarded this balance of responsibility and privilege.

The decencies of life forbid the intrusion into a person's private sphere and activities. Jewish law is firmly against prying into the affairs of others. For most people object to having their personal life exposed to others' gaze. Like other legal systems Jewish law has many rules whose object is to protect the individual's privacy. Indeed, the Jewish legislators were concerned about the dignity and propriety of life to which every individual was entitled.

2   Malachi 2,10
3   M. Megillah 4,3; S.A.O.H. 55,4; See Rabbi Dr. J. Rabbinowitz
    Mishnah Megillah p.114
4   Aboth 2,5

Many laws and regulations reflect the concern of the Rabbis for the well-being and independence of each individual. Thus, if a man wishes to build a wall in his courtyard he must build it at least four cubits away from his neighbour's window in order not to obstruct his light. If the window is low in the wall, the owner of the house can insist that he build the wall four cubits higher than the window so that no one can look into the house.[5] A neighbour's domestic affairs must be scrupulously respected. Gross intrusion into privacy is considered in the Halachah an harassment of a serious kind. A rabbinic dictum declares; "Damage caused to one by the lights of another is real damage".[6] Looking through one's window into the courtyard of another, where in ancient times the private affairs of an individual were conducted, or observing from a roof the domestic activities on a roof of an adjoining house, is a breach of privacy and constitutes an act of damage.[7]

These laws suggest that interference with a person's privacy constituted legal damage for which one could sue in court. While penalties for injuries and damages are exacted by the court only in cases where a clear act of damage or injury has been committed, interference with another's privacy itself constitutes a damaging act.

The Jewish jurists laid down rules and regulations defining the circumstances under which a person could legally claim that his peace at home was disturbed by the action of others. This right to peace and rest is stressed in the Mishnah.[8] Noise is one of the banes of modern living. But it was often a source of annoyance in ancient times.

5　M. Baba Bathra 2,4 and the discussion following in the Gemara.
6　Baba Bathra 2b
7　Ibid. 6b
8　Baba Bathra 2,3

Hence the Rabbis ruled that a person may protest against another who opens a shop within the courtyard. He can say to him "I cannot sleep because of the noise of those who go in and out". But none may protest against another and say "I cannot sleep because of the noise of the hammer or because of the noise of the millstone or because of the noise of children". The Talmud explains that "the noise of children" does not refer to the noise of children when they go into a shop to buy things but to the noise made by children in the school. Such noise could never become a ground for protest by next-door neighbours. The duty to educate children takes precedence over the individual's right to peace and quiet. Thus while neighbours can raise objections to the opening of a store in a residential courtyard because the traffic of the customers will disturb their peace, they cannot object to the opening of an elementary school by arguing that the noise of the children interferes with their rest.[9] Underlying this regulation was clearly the principle that the essential needs of the public, among which the religious education of the young plays a most vital part, take precedence over the comforts and amenities of the individual.

The Sages considered community solidarity vital in order to ensure the safety and religious well-being of the House of Israel. They expressed strong disapproval of individuals who isolated themselves from the community and failed to observe the *mitzvoth* of the Torah.[10] They cited Achan[11]: "Did not Achan the son of Zeraḥ commit a transgression concerning the devoted things and wrath

---

9   Baba Bathra 21a
10 Mechilta de Rabbi Simeon on Exodus 19,6
11 Joshua 22,20; Tanḥuma Nitzavim 2

fell upon all the congregation of Israel and that man perished not alone in his iniquity".

While zealous for the individual's freedom and independence the Jewish legislators insisted on his duty to obey religious authority and to adhere strictly to the rules and enactments of the community.

The enforcement of the law for the benefit of the public at large may sometimes conflict with the right of individual members. The aim and function of law is to dispense justice. It is for the judge to decide where the greater justice lies.

Jewish law not only insists on man's rights with respect to material possessions but also to his rights concerning his mental, intellectual and cultural achievements.

The invention of printing has been one of the most potent factors of modern civilisation. Jews with their devotion to study and learning welcomed the invention of printing with overwhelming enthusiasm and gratitude as an inestimable boon.[12] But, like other modern inventions, printing had presented many halachic problems.

The concept of ownership was not limited to things material. Literary works, pictures and manuscripts were included in it. The Biblical precept of "removing a neighbour's boundary"[13] was extended in the Halachah to the reprinting of books and the question of copyright. This question exercised the mind of R. Moses Isserls.[14] R. Meir Katzenellenbogen, known as Maharam Padwa

---

12 R. David Gans (1541-1613), the famous chronicler and historian, wrote finely and feelingly of the invention: "Blessed be He who bestowed upon man knowledge and taught him understanding". None of the former skills and inventions can compare with its importance. See Zemaḥ David, part 2; Offenbach, 1768 p.64
13 Deuteronomy 19,14
14 Isserls: Responsa 10

(of Padua), who served as Rabbi in Venice for a number of years and was acknowledged as one of the leading rabbinical authorities of his age, had lavished vast learning upon the preparation of an edition of Maimonides' Mishneh Torah with glosses and annotations. It appears that the conditions stipulated by the Gentile printer, were unacceptable to Katzenellenbogen. He then arranged with another printer to publish his work. The former printer promptly brought out a rival edition of the Mishneh Torah in the hope of ousting Katzenellenbogen's edition. The latter appealed to his kinsman, R. Moses Isserls, to forbid the sale of the infringing publication in Poland where the demand for such books must have been considerable. To Isserls this was a clear case of unfair competition. On this and other halachic grounds he pronounced a *herem* (ban) against the purchase of the new edition.

In his opinion it was a flagrant instance of הסגת גבול, unfair competition. Katzenellenbogen was certain to incur financial loss as the rival firm of publishers reduced the price. Among Isserls' halachic arguments we note his view that an accurate and reliable edition of a sacred work was not only proper but was required by Jewish law. Whilst concerned about the question of non-Jewish ill-feeling which his ban might cause, Isserls accepts the view of Tosafoth that in business affairs this fear does not apply. Of particular interest also is his contention, based on Talmudic teaching, that a Jewish scholar was entitled to support.

The question of copyright clearly engaged the minds of some of the halachic authorities. A later Halachist, the Hatam Sofer, concurred with Rema's opinion advancing an additional argument. The law of the land is binding in such matters and on the basis of this principle, he held that even in the absence of an express *herem* it is unlawful to reprint others' work without permission. He argued that the creative work of an author involving costs of publication, is his property. He no doubt refers to copyright and patent rights protected by the laws of modern states. It is a definite example of the application and development of the Halachah in changed conditions of society.[15]

It is sad to relate that the Katzenellenbogen case gave rise to a painful and prolonged conflict between the rival publishers and printers which finally and lamentably led to denunciation and discrimination resulting in the burning of the Talmud in 1554 by order of the Pope, as well as the closure of all Hebrew printing presses in Venice. The destruction and desecration of the sacred books followed by violent antisemitic propaganda could not but deeply affect the life, religious, cultural and social of Italian Jewry. Distressed by this event and deprived of Hebrew books it faced frustration and the threatening danger of the Torah being forgotten in its midst.[16]

The Halachah clearly relates to both the individual and the community. It lays stress not only upon the individual's responsibilities but also upon corporate solidarity and obligations. One Talmudic statement refers specifically to "community laws".[17] Quoting Isaiah[18] "The Lord hath broken the staff of the wicked, the sceptre of the rulers", this contains, said the Sages, an

15   Abodah Zarah 2a; Hatam Sofer H.M.41
16   Rabbi A. Siev, Hadorom 28, 1968 pp.183-184
17   Shabbath 139a
18   Isaiah 14,5

admonition to scholars not to teach such laws to ignorant judges.[19]

Another Talmudic dictum expresses the idea of communal solidarity. "All Israelites are guarantors for one another".[20] It is a dictum of wide-ranging import. It has reference to the consciousness of every individual that in his life and conduct he bears the responsibility not for himself alone but for his group, community and nation. The concept that all Israel are considered as one body, one entity, permeates many halachic rulings.

That the community bears a share of the responsibility for the sin of the individual is evident from the Torah.[21] "And they shall stumble one upon another as it were before the sword when none pursueth; and ye shall have no power to stand before your enemies". The Rabbis interpreted the verse to mean that they shall be responsible collectively for the sins of an individual member of the group.[22] They held that it was every man's duty to prevent wrongdoing by another.[23]

The idea of corporate dependence is enshrined in the ruling concerning the blessings to be recited before the performance of a *mitzvah*. Significantly, if one had already performed certain *mitzvoth* he could say the blessing for others.[24] The principle of ערבות, collective responsibility, underlies this rule. It may be explained

19 The reference, it has been suggested, is to communal officers appointed on occasion to oversee specific municipal institutions. See S. Belkin: In His Image, 9.123 Note 26
20 Shebuoth 39a כל ישראל ערבין זה בזה; Sotah 37b; Rosh Hashanah 29a, Rashi ad loc; Ritvo, Rosh Hashanah 29a, p. 25
הרי כל ישראל ערבין זה לזה וכלם כגוף אחד וכערב הפורע חוב חבירו
21 Leviticus 26,37
22 Sifra 12b and Tosefta Berakoth 4,16; Tanḥuma Vayigash 4
23 Sanhedrin 27b; Sotah 37b
24 S.A.O.Ḥ. 585,2

that since another Jew might not have fulfilled the obligation, a duty devolves upon a fellow-Jew to act on his behalf.

There are rules of conduct laid down in Jewish law, as in other systems of law, which are binding upon the community and can be enforced by the courts. The community as an entity has definite duties to its members. The Halachah recognizes the importance of community organization. It manifests some leniency respecting its administration. One example will serve. Discussions concerning religious observance as well as consideration of the accounts of the community are permitted on the Sabbath.[25] The attitude of the Halachah to essential public needs is evident from its lenient decisions in regard to the Intermediate Days of the Festivals.[26]

In order to ensure a high standard of honesty as well as complete confidence in philanthropic activity, charity must always be collected by two persons but its distribution requires a minimum of three.[27] Money collected for charitable purposes must be counted carefully, one coin at a time and not two at a time, lest people say that they take two and only count one.[28]

The Talmud attached great importance to community cohesion and solidarity, censuring solemnly those who dissociated themselves from the community. Two expressions attest to the Rabbis' attitude: "He who separates himself from the community" refers to an individual who stands aloof and shows no concern for

25 Shabbath 150a; S.A.O.Ḥ. 306,6
26 Moed Katan 4a-b
27 Baba Bathra 8b
28 Ibid.

community needs and welfare and "He who departs from the ways of the community" — who does not live in accordance with the law of the Torah.[29]

The community had a duty to appoint judges in every district and in every city.[30] Those who were charged with this task bore a heavy responsibility. Indeed, the Rabbis voiced strong criticism of those who appointed unworthy judges.[31]

Every Jewish community was obliged to have a Synagogue which was to be built on the higher part of the city.[32] Residents could compel the community leaders to erect a Synagogue. The *bimah* was to be in the centre[33] and there was to be a gallery for the women.[34] Peace and harmony was to reign in the Synagogue.[35] Quarrels in the Synagogue would lead to decline and fragmentation.[36] As the focal point of community life, the Synagogue served not only the religious needs of its members but also their social interests. It was the place for community worship and the source of Jewish spiritual life. As the expression of the Jewish genius it is the greatest institution of Judaism. It has helped to hallow the name of God and to preserve the Jewish tradition and way of life.

While the principal and primary responsibility for the education of children rested upon parents, the establishment of schools was also among the duties of the community. In the early half of the first century BCE

---

29 Ibid. 79a
30 Sanhedrin 16b; Tanḥuma Shoftim 5
31 Sanhedrin 7b. The Sages compared them with those who "Worshipped an Asherah".
32 Tanḥuma Beḥukotai 4
33 Sukkah 51b
34 Ibid.
35 Midrash Ḥazith 8
36 Ibid; Maimonides: Tefillah,11,1-21; S.A.O.Ḥ., 151,1-12

R. Simeon b. Shetaḥ created a school-system which was developed into a more comprehensive scheme by R. Joshua b. Gamala a few years shortly before the destruction of the Temple. A striking passage in the Talmud reads: "Remember for good the man named Joshua ben Gamala, because were it not for him the Torah would have been forgotten from Israel."[37] At first children were taught by their fathers and in consequence orphans were often deprived of religious instruction. It was thereupon resolved that teachers of children be appointed in Jerusalem. Finally, Joshua b. Gamala ordained that teachers should be appointed in every province and in every city and children about the age of six or seven were to be placed in their charge.[38] This is probably the earliest record of universal education in any country. Education was to be provided for all children regardless of the circumstances of the parents. The familar saying "Be careful of the children of the poor, since the Torah proceeds from them"[39] bears witness to the fact that the poor children of the community were not disadvantaged. There is ample evidence in the sources[40] that schools were common and that large numbers of pupils attended.

The deep desire and regard for knowledge made the provision of schools an essential obligation of each community. This duty also applied to adults, as the study of the Torah was not reserved only for students of jurisprudence. All Jews had to study the Torah as a religious duty and in order to carry out its precepts correctly.

37 Baba Bathra 21a
38 Ibid.
39 Nedarim 81a
40 J. Ḥagigah 1,7; Lamentations Rabbati,Introduction 2

Altogether the Halachah reflects a deep regard for the group and the community as well as its representatives;[41] To give one example: A mourner is not permitted to greet visitors during *shivah*. Nor may he engage in conversation with them. He is, however, allowed to do so out of respect for the representatives of the community.

The principle that all Israel are accountable for each other can be traced back to the Patriarchs who stood surety for Israel that they and their descendants would fulfil the commandments of the Torah.[42]

The introduction of the תקנה, ordinance, dates back to Talmudic times. The ordinances of R. Johanan b. Zakkai were of national and religious moment.[43] In ordaining general legal decrees the Rabbis took great care that these should not weigh heavily upon the majority of the community. They laid down the following principle: "We do not impose a decree upon the community unless the majority of the community can endure it".[44] Another rabbinic ruling, as mentioned before, was that a contemporary court could abolish the decree of an earlier court, only if it were superior to the former in knowledge and in numbers.[45] Tosafoth[46] and Maimonides[47] added the proviso that only if the decree of a former court had been accepted by the majority of the community. Their view was based on the principle that in a community which in all matters accepts the authority of the court but finds it impossible to conform to a particular decree, the

---

41 S.A.Y.D. 385 Rema
42 Tanhuma Vayiggash
43 Rosh Hashanah 29b
44 Baba Kamma 79b; Baba Bathra 60b
45 Gittin 36b; Abodah Zarah 36a
46 Tosafoth on Abodah Zarah 36a
47 Mamrim 2,2

will and welfare of that community must be further considered. This attitude reflects the concern of the Rabbis for the opinion and the sentiment of the public. Great care was to be taken never to burden it beyond its capacity.[48] This consideration reveals also the Rabbis' high concept of the status and authority of the communal organism. The Sages did not add a decree to another decree.[49]

Since Talmudic times the Synagogue embraced a wide range of activities in Jewish communal life. From a passage in the Jerusalem Talmud it would seem that an individual against whom a complaint was being made could be excluded from attending the Synagogue Service and thus call the attention of the community to a misdeed or grievance.[50] In the medieval communities there were no newspapers or journals. The Synagogue, the focal point of Jewish life, served also as a forum for the exposure of wrongs committed by individual members. Thus any Jew, who believed that he had a grievance against a fellow-Jew who had refused to obey the summons of the court, had a right to seek protection in the Synagogue until he had been given a public promise of redress. Yet the sacred spirit and decorum of the Synagogue prevented it from becoming a strident and uninhibited forum.[51] There was a concept that worship of God had to go hand in hand with justice to man. A sense of wrong and injustice would affect the fervour and quality of prayer. Isaiah warned against prayer offered by

---

48   Abodah Zarah 36a
49   Shabbath 21a; Yebamoth 109a
50   J. Kiddushin 61,7
51   Adret 4,56 This responsum is of particular interest as it casts light on the passage referred to in note 50, and on the Synagogue in medieval European communities.

those who were guilty of crime and murder. "And when ye make many prayers, I will not hear. Your hands are full of blood".[52] In these imperishable words the Prophet gave expression to God's rejection of prayer offered up by those guilty of misdeeds and heinous crimes.

As a legal sanction designed to protect the weak and oppressed against the powerful, the Synagogue reflected a strong sense of justice and righteousness. As a place of worship it hallowed, through its congregational prayers and meditations, God's name.[53] The prayers known as *Kaddish* and *Kedushah* which proclaim the sanctification of God's name are recited only in the presence of a congregation.

Deeply conscious and proud of their own legal system, revealed in the Torah and the tradition which they helped to create and hand down, the Rabbis strongly warned Jews against resorting to Gentile courts. Such action would cause defamation of the Name of God.[54]

In the Middle Ages celebrated Halachists representing the French and Spanish Jewish communities solemnly affirmed the attitude of the Sages in urging Jews to refrain from submitting cases to Gentile civil courts. Accordingly they introduced ordinances which forbade Jews to litigate before Gentile tribunals.[55]

The ordinances were generally enforced by means of the *herem* which was a powerful weapon vested in the leadership. Its aim was to maintain law and order and discipline in Jewish life. In its harsher form the *herem* involved total ostracism, a complete moral, religious and

52   Isaiah 1,15
53   Megillah 23b; Berakoth 21b
54   Gittin 88b
55   Adret 6,254; 5,287; 2,290;

social boycott of the offender. He was barred from joining in any synagogal service. Disobedience of the ḥerem could result in a fine, monetary or personal. The ḥerem was usually effective in compelling adherence to communal regulations. It was designed to uphold the moral and social standards and values of the community.

The Rabbis had great respect for religious usage, מנהג.[56] Often when in difficulty concerning what the proper halachic decision should be they accepted the established practice of the community as authoritative. Of special significance in this respect is the Talmudic principle: "If an *halachah* is indefinite the rabbinic advice was contained in the dictum — 'Go forth and see what the community is accustomed to do, then conduct yourself accordingly'."[57] This statement of the Jerusalem Talmud indicates that when the court is uncertain about the application of a particular law or regulation it can safely rely on the practice of the community in the assurance that such practice is based upon a former halachic decree or interpretation of the law. It is an eloquent and convincing expression of faith that the prevailing usages of a community are rooted in halachic traditions and norms even if these are unknown to a contemporary court.

As has been observed, both the individual and the community have their respective duties and rights in Jewish law. In a dispute between the minority or an individual and the community, *Kahal,* the latter could compel a minority of members to abide by its decision. This principle is based on the general Talmudic rule of the power of the majority which allows the members of a

56   M. Sukkah 3,11; M. Baba Metzia 7,1; Erubin 14b
57   J. Peah 7,5

community to introduce regulations for measures, prices and wages and prescribe punishment for their infringement.[58]

In the early part of the 18th century R. Zevi Hirsch b. Jacob Ashkenazi, known as the Ḥacham Zevi, ruled in Amsterdam that the *Kahal* may avail itself of the power of the secular court to enforce its decisions, but only after it received the consent of the Beth Din.[59]

In a dispute between the *Kahal* and an individual, the *Kahal* may confiscate the individual's property in order to ensure his appearance before a Beth Din. From this ruling it is evident that the *Kahal* and the individual alike were under the jurisdiction of the Beth Din, whose power and prestige were high and widely acknowledged.

The extensive power of the Beth Din and the *Kahal* derived, according to Rabbenu Tam, from the ruling of Mar Samuel: דינא דמלכותא דינא — "The law of the State is binding". The court had the right to declare private property as *res nullius*, ownerless, a power limited to civil matters.[60]

Some held that the legal maxim הפקר בית דין הפקר applies in matters that are in the public interest even if it does not serve as a defensive measure.[61] The earlier authorities argue that we only apply this principle if it serves as a defensive measure sustaining a Biblical command. Reference has already been made to the *prozbul*, Hillel's innovative legal device based, according to a Talmudic view, on the principle of הפקר בית דין הפקר.[62]

---

58   Baba Bathra 8b
59   Responsum 14
60   Baba Kamma 113a; Maimonides' Commentary to the Mishnah Nedarim 3,3
61   Encyclopedia Talmudit vol. 10 p.108
62   Deuteronomy 15,9; Gittin 36a

Not only the individual but also the community enjoyed property rights. Yet communal ownership of property appears to differ from that of joint holders. A public thoroughfare may serve as a good example. It belongs to the inhabitants of the town. Yet the inhabitants are not like partners, שותפין.

The Mishnah distinguishes between the community ציבור and joint holders in connection with substituted offerings.[63] For the community, it has been argued, is a distinct entity, even a legal entity, and has an existence over and above that of the individual members of which it is comprised.[64] The late Rav Kook, too, held the view that the property owned by a community of Israel is to be regarded as jointly owned property.[65]

That the Rabbis accorded the community a distinct legal status testifies to their attitude to the corporate nature of the congregation and its specific needs, social, religious, educational, public health and safety. All communal offices, even that of physicians, were subject to the endorsement of the court and the approval of the community. The governing board who conducted the administration were to pay due regard to the opinion of the members of the community.

The education of children; the apportionment of communal taxes according to strict rules; the acquisition and sale of communal property — all came within the scheme of the community organization, supervised by the

---

63 Temurah 1,6
64 See Rabbi K. Kahana: Naḥlat Kohen pp 79-84. He quotes R. Joseph
    Rosen (1858-1936), known as the Rogachover Gaon, who holds that
    partnership and community are different and distinct concepts. Rabbi
    Kahana concludes that in most respects the community is a distinct
    entity.
65 Responsa: Mishpat Kohen on Mitzvot Hateluyot Baaretz 12

governing board. Indeed, the entire religious, social and commercial life of the community, including exact weights and measures, the price of food and the rate of wages,were all controlled by the community.

Communal property was allowed to be bought and sold by its representatives. The Codes, however, restrain the exercise of this power. Thus a Synagogue may be sold in order to build a Beth Hamidrash, or to buy Scrolls of the Law but not conversely.[66]

In Judaism the poor have a claim upon charity, and the problem of poor relief occupied the minds of the communal leaders. Humanitarian considerations governed the entire scheme of charitable activity. These are reflected in Jewish legislation. Interestingly, while Caro introduced the laws of Passover with the Talmudic requirement[67] to expound these laws thirty days before the festival, Isserls adds: "It is the custom to buy wheat and to distribute it among the poor for Passover". Isserls' gloss is based on a passage in the Jerusalem Talmud.[68] In his deep concern for the needs of the poor, the Rema felt that the period of thirty days before Passover should not only be devoted to study of the many and complex laws of Passover but also to the duty of the communities to provide for the poor.

There was always the fear that charity, instead of alleviating distress, might affect the self-respect of the recipient. This would increase the suffering it was intended to relieve. In the case of support for the poor for Passover it was laid down that they should be given the opportunity to arrange for the baking of their own

66   Megillah 26b; S.A.O.Ḥ. 153,1
67   Pesaḥim 6a; S.A.O.Ḥ. 429,1 Rema
68   J. Baba Bathra 1,4

matzoth in the communal bakery as was the practice of the better placed members of the community.

Such feeling for the sensitivities of the poor reflects the attitude of Jewish law to charity and to those who are to benefit from it. For Jewish philanthropy was inspired by humanitarian and social motives. Every citizen was to contribute towards the needs of the poor not merely as one individual helping another individual but as a member of a group with a corporate obligation. In this way the recipient would feel less embarrassed than by receiving relief from another person. Indeed, as early as Talmudic times, provision was made by Jewish communities for the support of the poor. The assessment of members' contributions for charitable purposes was among the essential tasks of the communities.[69] It is informative that the Code devotes thirteen chapters to the laws of charity.[70]

The redemption of captives became early a primary religious duty of Jewish communities. The anguish that attends captivity, the Talmud declares, is the most distressing and agonizing of all human suffering.[71] Referring to Jeremiah's words,[72] "And it shall come to pass if they say to you, whither shall we go forth, then thou shalt tell them, thus saith the Lord: such as are for death, to death; and such as are for the sword, to the sword; and such as are for the famine, to the famine; and such as are for the captivity, to the captivity", the Rabbis commented: "Captivity is harder than all other punishments for all sufferings are included in it."[73] The

69 Baba Bathra 10a
70 S.A.Y.D. 247-259
71 Baba Bathra 8,b
72 Jeremiah 15,2
73 Baba Bathra 8,b

release from captivity was therefore regarded as the greatest service a Jew could render to a fellow-Jew and to God. Thus the individual and the community were enjoined to do everything possible to secure the release of those held in captivity. No community, however poor, would wish to evade this responsibility. Indeed, no ransom was too burdensome or high if it were to secure the captive's freedom.

In Jewish history cases of captivity were unfortunately too frequent and communities found it imperative to establish special funds for the purpose of ransoming fellow-Jews. So important and urgent was this duty that the Halachah permitted funds designated for other communal and religious needs to be diverted for this purpose. Even a fund raised for the specific object of building a synagogue could, in special circumstances, be allocated to this end.[74] Whenever a situation arose for which the available funds were inadequate a special levy would be imposed upon the members of the community.[75]

The readiness of Jewish communities to pay any price as ransom for a captured brother-Jew at times served to encourage kidnappers in their criminal activities demanding substantial and even extortionate sums. The Rabbis, therefore, felt impelled to restrict the amounts to be paid. In the words of the Talmud: "Captives should not be ransomed for more than their value in the interest of the general welfare."[76] It must be added that the rabbinic restriction with respect to ransom applied to a community only.[77] An individual or the captive's family

74   S.A.Y.D. 252,1
75   Baba Bathra 8a-b
76   Gittin 45a
77   Ibid.; S.A.Y.D. 252,1

was permitted to pay even a high ransom in order to secure his freedom.[78]

Maimonides speaks of this duty in very solemn tones. "He who shirks this obligation", he writes, "transgresses the commandment of the Torah: 'Thou shalt not harden thine heart nor close thy hand' as well as the commandment 'Thou shalt not rule with vigour over him in thy sight'. Delay in the effort to redeem captives is tantamount to bloodshed".[79]

The Rabbis forbade assisting captives in their desire to escape lest the captors take revenge upon the inhabitants of the place or subject the remaining captives to torture.[80] Jews who had experienced the horrors and agonies of captivity considered no price too high to secure a fellow-man's liberty.

Before and after the destruction of the Temple in 70 CE many Jews were sold as slaves by the Romans. In the Middle Ages, too, some rulers imprisoned important Jewish persons demanding high ransoms for their release. The celebrated R. Meir of Rothenburg was imprisoned by the Emperor Rudolph who demanded a high ransom from the Jewish community. R. Meir did not permit the community to meet the Emperor's demand. He quoted the Talmudic ruling to which reference has already been made. He thought that the community's willingness to pay would encourage further acts of blackmail.[81]

The classical sources testify to the active participation

78 Rosh on Ketuboth 52a
79 Matnoth Aniyyim 8,10
80 Gittin 45a
81 E.E. Urbach: The Tosaphists, Their History, Writings and Methods pp 426-427

of the community in both the joys and sorrows of the individual. Thus the prayers known as Vehu Raḥum and Taḥnun are omitted in the statutory morning and afternoon Services, in the presence of an individual who celebrates a joyful event. The congregation must refrain from uttering these solemn and moving petitions which may affect the person's felicitous mood. These prayers are likewise not recited in a house of mourning. They tell of Israel's sufferings and martyrdom and would add to the mourner's grief. The worshippers also pray in them to God for personal needs and hopes. The recital of these prayers might detract from the congregation's sympathy for the bereaved individuals.[82] The lenient attitude of the Halachah to these liturgical rules reveals its deep humanity.

The question of the freedom of the individual and the authority of the community is indeed complex. The individual, it has been rightly said, represents in himself a world of his own. The Halachah accords him status and importance. "A single man was created in the world", the Sages said, "to teach that if anyone caused a single life to perish Scripture regards it as though he had caused an entire world to perish". Similarly, if anyone saves the life of a single individual Scripture accounts to him as though he had saved an entire world.[83]

Again, a single man, they declared, was created for the sake of peace among men, that none should say to his fellow, "My father was greater than thy father". Therefore every man must say, "For my sake was the world created."[84] The doctrine of human rights, now

82 S.A.O.Ḥ. 131,4
83 M. Sanhedrin 4,5
84 Ibid.

widely acknowledged, even if not universally practised, flows from this moral concept.

While the Jewish jurists were concerned about the unity and integrity of the community they were equally strong in their advocacy of the freedom and independence of the individual. The general duties an individual owed to others clearly imposed a limitation on his freedom. His right to privacy is emphasized in the Halachah.[85] The Sages showed a lenient attitude to the actions of saintly men who on occasion did not seem to adhere strictly to the law. Two examples spring to mind. Because they were convinced of Honi's saintliness they did not show disapproval of his actions.[86] Todos of Rome was an important and influential man whose piety and observance were not in doubt. Although he acted contrary to a ritual practice, the Rabbis refrained in his case from exercising their authority and sanction.[87] In maintaining the religious and social life strict communal order and discipline were deemed crucial. Unfettered freedom of the individual would result in religious and communal chaos.

The injunction to follow the majority opinion of the religious leaders has ensured the uniformity of the law which is essential to the people's religious and national health. To this law all must adhere strictly.[88] Maimonides[89] ruled that regarding laws which are deduced or expounded by the method of "minor to major" if all the members of the Highest Court are unanimous there can be no argument, but if they are

85   S.A.H.M. 153-156
86   M. Taanith 3,8; Ibid. 23a
87   Pesahim 53a
88   Sefer Ha-Hinuch 78; 495-496
89   Mamrim 1,3

divided in their opinions the law is decided according to the majority. In regard to decrees, ordinances and customs, if there is a division of opinion as to the need for their introduction, the questions are to be deliberated by the two sides and the opinion of the majority prevails.

All the needs of the community are to be provided for, declares an ancient source,[90] subject to the agreement of the majority of the community who always had to be guided by the Talmudic ruling, already mentioned, that "no decree which the majority of the community finds impossible to endure" should be issued.[91]

The enforcement of communal ordinances and enactments was also subject to the rule of the majority. According to R. Eliezer b. Joel Halevi, known as the Rabiah,[92] the majority could impose their will upon the minority who did not agree to the ordinances. The Rosh[93] explains: "The principle of the rule of the majority אחרי רבים להטות is indicated in the Torah. It should apply to matters appertaining to the community and if the community agreed upon a certain question no individual may oppose it. For no community could decide on any action that would be acceptable to every member".

The Rabiah lays down the principle that the Communal Board, consisting of the "Seven Best Men" שבעה טובי העיר, had in their local community as much power in civil matters as the Sanhedrin had over all Israel.

It would seem from the sources that after the Supreme Judicial Tribunal and religious leadership had ceased, the

90 Tosefta Sanhedrin 2,13
91 Horayoth 3b
92 Quoted in the Responsa of R. Ḥayyim Or Zarua 222
93 Responsa, Kelal 6,5

community assumed the supremacy, authority and legislative power. Thus Adret[94] says: "No one has a right to reject or refuse to recognize the communal enactments." He further declares:[95] "The individual is to the community what the communities were to the Highest Court".

In the democracy of the community the general body of members constituted the highest organ. They appointed their representatives as well as the Dayanim of the Beth Din. While the rule of the majority prevailed, the Rabbis were concerned to protect the rights of the minority in the community. At the same time they took care to ensure that the minority could not impede or hinder actively or by a passive attitude the work and progress of the community.[96]

It is evident from the sources that the Halachists recognized the wide autonomy of the Jewish communities without which they could not arrange their internal activities or decide on the type of organization suitable to them. This freedom was, however, subject to one proviso: that nothing they did would conflict with the principles of Jewish law and the basic tenets of justice. All religious matters were under the jurisdiction of the Beth Din. A communal enactment which was in conflict with the Halachah had no validity.

Sanctions were instituted to ensure obedience to the various rabbinic and communal ordinances. Some of these sanctions were not always widely received.[97] The ordinance of Rabbenu Gershom banning polygamy was

94 Responsa 7,490
95 Ibid. 3,438 and 5,126
96 S.A.Ḥ.M. 5
97 S.A.Y.D. 334

accepted and has remained binding until the present time. It was so accepted because the enactment was in basic harmony with the spirit of Jewish law and morality and fulfilled a high social purpose among the people. The Talmud makes reference to different degrees in sanctions.[98] The *herem* is no doubt the most serious and stringent.[99] Maimonides sets out the laws contained in the Babylonian and Jerusalem Talmudim relating to sanctions. He declares, "Although a scholar is permitted to excommunicate a person who has offended against him it is not proper that he should do so. He should rather shut his eyes to the words of the ignorant and not pay heed to them."[100]

There were sanctions against those who caused dissension and indulged in slander.[101] Those who denigrated scholars or showed no respect for them provoked the severe criticism and condemnation of the Sages.[102]

The Rabbis censured communal leaders who exercised their functions with arrogance. Indeed, leaders were to act with humility and reverence. Divine retribution would be meted out to communal officers who put the congregation in fear for other than religious reasons. They were equally warned against conducting the affairs of the community lightheartedly. Nor were leaders to stride over the heads of the holy people though they be ordinary and humble folk. For they are the children of Abraham, Isaac and Jacob.[103]

98　Moed Katan 16b and 17a
99　Berakoth 19a; See Dr. Isidore Epstein: The Responsa of Rabbi Simon b. Zemaḥ Duran pp. 69-70
100　Talmud Torah 7,13; S.A.Y.D. 334,45
101　Responsa Radbaz, Part 6,21
102　Shabbath 119b; Baba Bathra 75a; Koheleth Rabbati 9,26
103　Rosh Hashanah 17a; Maimonides: Sanhedrin 25,1

Reflecting on the record of the Jewish communities in the Diaspora, alluded to in this study, one cannot but be profoundly impressed by their energy, courage and tenacity. Refugees from persecution and discrimination, they succeeded in founding in their new surroundings Synagogues, Battei Din and institutions devoted to education, philanthropy and social welfare. What vouchsafed their vitality and cohesion was clearly their inner spiritual strength, willpower and discipline. Believing in the supremacy of the Halachah they organized their community life according to its distinctive fabric with its strands of faith, hope and humanity. It is a record richly meaningful and immensely moving.

CHAPTER SIX

HUMAN RELATIONS

The belief in the dignity and worth of the human personality governs the relations, social and economic, of one individual to another. The rules formulated in Jewish law provide for right behaviour and honest dealing in trade and commerce, in personal and public relations. They demonstrate the Jewish moral and religious principles underlying day to day conduct in all departments of life.

Significantly, six of the Ten Commandments relate to precepts concerning duties we owe to our fellow men. The Golden Rule "Thou shalt love thy neighbour as thyself"[1] was deemed by the Sages as an all-embracing doctrine upon which the entire moral structure of the Torah rests.

Isaiah, in speaking of true and false worship, stresses the importance of right conduct in human relations. In imperishable words he gave forceful expression to his conviction that the Divine government of the world was based upon morality, justice and truth. He denounced, in words of fire, the evils of his time,

1 Leviticus 19,18

superstition, drunkenness, greed, bribery and corruption.[2]

When R. Akiba declared that this precept is the great principle of the Torah,[3] he meant to convey that all the duties that man owes to his fellowmen are comprehended in this rule. The furtherance of interest, care and compassion among men is its ultimate objective. The welfare of others must concern man as much as his own welfare.

Maimonides formulated the Golden Rule of the Torah as follows: "All the things that you wish others to do to you, do you to others."[4] Indeed, this teaching was to serve as the motive for all human relations and for the betterment of society.

The Halachah provides, among others, the following practical examples of the Golden Rule. It insists that the injunction of the Torah applies even to a man guilty of the most serious crime and condemned to death. The Sages exhorted the court to choose for him a less painful death to ease his suffering and agony.[5]

Consideration for others is shown by the rule of helping a fellowman to unload or load heavy burdens whether it be for a friend or enemy.[6] It exempted old and distinguished scholars from this duty as such work would be beyond their physical capacity and strength. It would not be in keeping with their status and dignity.[7]

2   Isaiah, 1,10-27
3   Sifra on Leviticus 19.18
4   Sefer Ha-Mitzvoth, Soncino ed. Vol. 1, 206
5   Sanhedrin 45a
6   Mechilta on Exodus 23,5; M. Baba Metzia 2,10
7   Mechilta de R. Simeon b. Yoḥai on Exodus 23,5; Baba Metzia 32b

The Biblical prohibition, "Thou shalt not go up and down as a talebearer among thy people"[8] forbids the spreading of tales, even if they are true, concerning the deeds of a neighbour. The Rabbis warn earnestly against the seriousness of the offence of circulating evil reports against others.[9] Maimonides likewise condemns those who convey information harmful to another person's reputation.[10] The Rabbis' vigorous censure of this offence is seen from the fact that they compare it to the denial of the existence of God.[11]

Mutual responsibility requires that one rebuke a fellowman who is about to do anything which is an infringement of the law. The verse, "Thou shalt surely rebuke thy neighbour"[12] contains also the doctrine of unity and solidarity expressed by the Rabbis in a familiar teaching, "All Israel are guarantors for each other".[13] This basic principle emphasizes the responsibilities of the individual Jew. He must be as concerned about the good name and conduct of fellow Jews as about his own.

The laws relating to compensation for injuries sustained reflect powerfully the recognition of the Sages of the worth of the individual. Where human life or bodily injury were involved all victims were alike. No man is superior to another.[14] He who wounds his fellowman becomes culpable on five counts: for injury, pain, healing, loss of time and for indignity inflicted.

---

8   Leviticus 19,16
9   Shabbath 56b; Pesaḥim 87b and 118a; J. Peah 16a
10 Deoth 5,2
11 Arachin 15b
12 Leviticus 19,17
13 Shebuoth 39a; Sanhedrin 27b
14 Maimonides: Ḥobel U-Mazik 2,11; Baba Kamma 85b

Man was created in the image of God and his dignity, his character and his rights were to be respected. To inflict indignity upon any man was one of the most serious offences.[15] In R. Akiba's opinion the value and worth of the human personality was indeed high.[16]

The right of every individual to respect, dignity and freedom also imposes upon him responsibilities towards others, their persons, their property and their privacy. Jewish law forbids the establishment of businesses which may cause unpleasant odours to the people of the town. Accordingly, a tannery may be set up only in a part of the town where the inconvenience produced by the tanning of hides will be minimal.[17] Likewise a person may not build a permanent threshing-floor within his own grounds unless his site extends over fifty cubits in each direction ensuring that the wind will not carry the chaff and injure his neighbours.[18] Although legally a person cannot be held responsible for injuries caused by chaff blown by the wind, morally it was considered a serious offence. Maimonides[19] says that it comes under the category of doing damage with one's arrow.

In the opinion of the Rabbis an individual is not permitted to exercise his personal and property rights if they interfere, even indirectly, with another's domestic affairs, comfort and peace of mind.

The Torah enjoins respect for the privacy of the individual regardless of his station in life.[20] "When

15 M. Baba Kamma 8,3
16 Ibid. 8,6
17 M. Baba Bathra 2,9
18 Ibid. 2,8
19 Shechenim 11,1
20 Deuteronomy 24, 10-11

thou dost lend thy neighbour any manner of loan thou shalt not go into his house to fetch his pledge. Thou shalt stand without and the man to whom thou dost lend shall bring forth the pledge without unto thee." While a person may be in need of your help you must not do anything that may embarrass him or detract from his human dignity. Help must be given graciously and must never invade the home-life of the person in need of assistance.

If an article of clothing was also used as a bed-covering and was given by the debtor to the creditor as a pledge, the latter was enjoined to return the garment at nightfall and not deprive the former of a necessity of life. In the words of the Psalmist, "Happy is he that considereth the poor."[21]

The sources relating to neighbours and their rights bear testimony to the importance the Halachah showed for just human relations. The mutual responsibilities governing human behaviour in day-to-day activities are set out in great detail. Of particular importance is the law that stresses the legal and moral obligations that a man owes to his neighbours. Those closest to him, whether by kinship or proximity, have the first call on him. This principle applies both to charity as well as business interests. A passage in the Mechilta reads; "If a poor man and a rich man stand before thee....even to the poor with thee."[22] The Sages took these words to apply to the poor who are near you.

The law governing the sale of property reflects the rights of adjoining neighbours, rights designed to ensure equitable conduct, peace and harmony.

21   Exodus 22,25-26; Psalm 41,2
22   Mechilta on Exodus 22,25

Accordingly, if one is about to sell property the neighbour whose property is adjacent has the legal right of pre-emption.[23] The Rabbis found Biblical support for this rule in the verse "And thou shalt do what is right and good in the sight of the Lord".[24] It is clear that this duty was not enjoined as a moral duty only but as a legal obligation. Thus if a property was sold contrary to this rule, the adjacent neighbour had a right to offer the purchase price and evict the first buyer.

The Rabbis strongly condemned unfair competition in business relations. The following Talmudic comment is their commendation of those who scrupulously forebore from encroaching upon another's preserves.[25] Interpreting the words of Ezekiel,[26] "Neither has he defiled his neighbour's wife," the Sages applied the Prophet's words to him who had no design on his neighbour's trade or profession.

To the Sage, R. Phinehas ben Jair, who was known for his profound piety and impeccable honesty, the Talmud attributes many miracles. One tells how once while he was on his way to the academy the River Ginai which he had to cross divided and he passed through on dry ground.[27] His pupils, who had followed him asked if they might, without danger, cross the river in the same way. R. Phinehas answered "Only those who have never offended any one may do so". There are different kinds of offence or pain that are caused to others. There is offence, where both parties are right

23 Baba Bathra 26a
24 Deuteronomy 24,10-11
25 Sanhedrin 81a
26 Ezekiel 18,10
27 J. Demai I,3; Ḥullin 7a

and the offence is the result of business competition. Neither party has transgressed the law, yet one has caused offence and suffering to another. The attitude of the Sage was that if his pupils had caused any sort of distress to a fellowman, even if justice was on their side, the miracle would not be vouchsafed to them. He believed that a miracle was to inspire in man an awareness of God. Those who lacked moral sensitivity would not benefit from the lesson of a miracle.

The concept of human freedom is implicit in Jewish thought and legislation. Interpreting the words[28] "For unto Me the children of Israel are servants" the Rabbis commented "and not servants to servants".[29] The idea of freedom clearly lies behind many of the regulations governing the relationship between employer and employee.

The worker who hired himself out for the day has the right to terminate his engagement at any time provided he could be replaced with no financial loss to the employer.[30] In some places the employer had to provide meals for the employee, the menu for which was regulated. It included, in some instances, dainty dishes.[31] This was an extension of the Biblical law which entitled the labourer to eat of the produce on which he happened to be engaged, even an amount exceeding his wages. The Rabbis, however, urged workmen not to be greedy as they might find the doors of employers closed to them.[32]

The attitude of the Sages to the rights of the employee is reflected in their interpretation of the Scriptural

28   Leviticus 25,55
29   Baba Metzia 10a
30   Ibid. 7a-b
31   Ibid. 88a-b
32   Ibid. 92a

verse.[33] "Judah is gone into exile because of affliction and because of great servitude". It referred to those who deprived the worker of his wages.[34]

The concern of the Rabbis for the rights of workmen is forcefully expressed in the Mishnah.[35] "One who engages labourers and demands that they commence early or that they work late - where local usage is not to commence early or late - he may not compel them. Where it is the practice to supply food (to one's labourers) he must supply them therewith. Everything depends on local custom...."

That a workman may opt out in the middle of the day stems no doubt from his fundamental right to personal freedom and independence. To deny him this right would be tantamount to subjecting him to his employer against his own will. However, the right of the labourer in regard to retraction is not absolute. He is not permitted, for example, to free himself from his contractual responsibility in order to secure employment elsewhere at a higher rate of payment.[36]

Workmen's wages were fixed by the authorities who safeguarded the employees' standard of life. There were also regulations as to the hours of labour and other rights. In some communities rules were laid down by unions of artisans who were permitted to call a period of rest (strike) in defence of their rights.[37] The working hours were also fixed. The time taken up by the workman in going to the place of labour was included in the

33   Lamentations 1,3
34   Lamentations Rabbati 1,29
35   Baba Metzia 7,1
36   S.A.Ḥ.M. 333,4 Rema
37   Tosefta Baba Metzia 11,25; Baba Metzia 77a

working hours but not the time needed by the labourer to return to his home.[38] Even if the employer paid the workman more than the usual rate of wages he was not allowed to make him work longer hours. If longer hours were specially agreed it implied that the increase was for his skill in executing better work and not in respect of longer hours.[39] If the employee undertook to perform work that required immediate attention and postponement of which would result in irretrievable loss, he could not retract without incurring a penalty.[40]

Believing that every man regardless of his social status was entitled to freedom and independence, the Rabbis enjoined on the employer to show kindness and compassion in the treatment of his employee. He was not to deprive him of any enjoyment lest he feel inferior to his employer.[41] The Sages showed high regard for those whom they engaged to work for them.[42] They required the same standard of their employees. According to a Talmudic ruling the workman's wages must be adequate for his family's needs.[43] This ruling shows the concern of the Sages for the welfare of the workman who deserved proper reward for his labour.

But in the relationship between employer and employee there must be mutual honesty. There must not be one-sided duties and responsibilities. Workmen equally owe integrity and loyalty to their employers. The time for which they were hired was not their own. To waste an employer's time would amount to robbery.

38 Baba Metzia 83b
39 Ibid. 83a
40 Maimonides: Sechiruth 9,4; S.A.H.M. 333,5
41 Kiddushin 22a referring to Leviticus 25,40 and Deuteronomy 15,16
42 J. Baba Kamma 8,6 with reference to Job 31,15
43 Ketuboth 105a

Accordingly, workers were exempt from the performance of certain religious obligations where this would interfere with their work. The time of their hire belonged to their employers.[44] They were to curtail the recital of Grace after Meals.[45] Nor were they required to descend for the reading of the Morning Shema from a tree or scaffolding on which they happened to be working. They could recite it where they were. "Craftsmen may read the Shema on the top of a tree or on the top of a course of stones".[46] Employees were not allowed to deny themselves food as they might be too weak to carry out their work efficiently.[47] Workmen were not allowed to retain the remnants of material for themselves but a tailor was permitted to retain a piece of cloth that did not exceed the size of three handbreadths.[48]

The relationship between employer and employee stresses strongly the Jewish concept that the life of every individual is a sacred trust over which no one can exercise unfettered power or authority. It is a relationship which is governed by the principle of equity and fairness and is in the nature of a contract which must be scrupulously honoured by both parties.

An extension of the Biblical injunction[49] relating to the gratuity, הענקה, payable by the master to his Hebrew servant when he was set free, is the basis for general compensation for workmen. A reference in the thirteenth century Sefer Ha-Ḥinuch[50] reads: "This precept applied to

44   Baba Metzia 78a
45   Berakoth 46a
46   Ibid. 16a האומנין קורין בראש האילן או בראש הנדבך
47   S.A.Ḥ. M. 337,19
48   Baba Kamma 119 a-b
49   Deuteronomy 15, 12-14
50   Sefer Ha-Ḥinuch 450

both male and female during Temple times.... Nevertheless, even in these days the wise should take heed and act with additional moral insight. Should he hire a servant for a long or even a short period, he should bestow liberal gifts upon him when he leaves his service from that with which God, may He be blessed, had blessed him".

Later scholars recognized this duty of the employer as legally binding. In Jewish law, they argued, the status of the Hebrew slave was like that of a hired workman.[51] Others were of the opinion that the general workman's compensation can be derived from the Scriptural exhortation,[52] "That thou mayest walk in the way of good men and keep the paths of the righteous". They compared it with the incident recorded in the Talmud.[53] The statement of the Sefer Ha-Ḥinuch indicates that the intention of the Torah was to make the employer concerned for the worker's future. He should not leave his service empty-handed. For justice, equality and truth must pervade all human relations.

It is a salutary commentary that amid prejudice, discrimination and persecution to which Jews have so often been subjected, ethical principles and ideals have continued to motivate their individual and corporate life.

---

51   Deuteronomy 15,18; Kiddushin 22b
52   Proverbs 2,20
53   Baba Metzia 83a

CHAPTER SEVEN

LENIENCY AND TOLERANCE

Leniency and tolerance characterize many rabbinic rulings and enactments. Ancient oral traditions, the immutable principles of the Halachah, and the creative methods of interpretation of the Sages combined to enable them to penetrate the truth and intention of the Torah.

Significantly, in addition to the legal devices introduced by the Jewish jurists in order to preserve the law, as I had occasion to indicate earlier, in cases of crucial need, they resorted to what is known as הוראת שעה "a decision of the hour". It was only in extraordinary situations that they felt impelled to pronounce in accordance with this prerogative. The Sages could exercise such a prerogative without affecting the principles. Even in capital cases they would dispense with certain procedural requirements and convict. One example out of many will suffice to explain the circumstances in which a celebrated Sage felt that the need of the hour justified special rulings. Simeon b. Shetaḥ had executed by hanging eighty women in one day in Ashkelon. This was in conflict with the law which did not permit more than one capital case to be dealt with on one day. Nor was hanging a mode of execution in the case of women.[1] But it was a decision prompted by the exigencies of the time which demanded drastic action in order to eradicate witchcraft from Israel.

The court could impose punishments not only in cases of the infringement of the law but as a defensive measure in order to protect the law.[2]

The social and economic relations between Jew and Gentile are dealt with in the sources. Restrictions and limitations are laid down in the Talmud[3] in respect of both the time for transacting business and the type of business deals that Jews were permitted to conduct with Gentiles.

In the Middle Ages the Halachists also manifested a lenient approach. "For three days before the festivals of Gentiles," the Mishnah states, "Jews are forbidden to have business dealings with them, to lend to them or borrow from them, to pay them or be repaid by them."[4] R. Menaḥem Meiri held that Christians and Moslems need not be included among the idolaters and accordingly could be exempt from the prohibition. He says, "In these times no one heeds these warnings at all, (even during their festival days) not even a rabbi, a scholar, a disciple or a pious man".[5] And some of the commentators gave the reason..."since the community cannot endure such restrictions for we have to have business dealings with them because of our livelihood. In our times it is impossible for the community to adhere to

---

1   M. Sanhedrin 6,4; J. Sanhedrin 6,9;
2   Maimonides: Sanhedrin 24,4; Tur S.A.Ḥ.M. 2,1
3   Abodah Zarah 2a ff
4   Ibid. Tosafoth ad loc.
5   Abodah Zarah, Beth Ha-Beḥira ed. A. Schreiber. 1944, pp.39,46,591

the Mishnaic prohibition".[6] Conditions had radically changed and the contemporary Halachist took account of the times.

Meiri discusses another Mishnaic ruling which forbids Jews to sell arms to non-Jews. Yet the Gemara permits it. He explains that they use the arms to protect the city and its inhabitants against any attack. He extended this permission, as did other Halachists, to sell various commodities because wherever a man finds hospitality and protection he must do his utmost to show gratitude to his hosts. For this very reason a moderate approach has been allowed in relations with Gentiles, many of whom work with or for Jews in different spheres of business.

The Sages manifested a lenient attitude regarding a דבר האבוד, work the non-performance of which would entail financial loss. Such work was permitted in certain circumstances when at other times it would be forbidden. This ruling applies to cases involving both ritual and civil matters. Accordingly, work which could not be done before Passover or Sukkoth was permitted to be performed on the intermediate weekdays of these Festivals. Similarly, in exceptional conditions the observance of the seven day period of mourning in the matter of work, the non-performance of which would cause a loss such as the mourner could not afford, the law was relaxed.

The loss of ideas or of interpretation comes under the concept of דבר האבוד. It would therefore be permitted to write down intellectual reflections on the Intermediate Days.

---

6 Naḥmanides, Abodah Zarah Novellae 13a cf. Ritvo ibid. 6b

In any estimate of the humanity of Jewish law the principle of considerable loss must receive attention. It relates to ritual matters and according to some authorities it comes under the category of emergency cases. This principle permits a lenient decision when the strict application of the law would cause considerable loss and prove a hardship. It was first introduced by R. Moses Mintz (15th century) and is based on the Talmudic sentiment expressed in the saying, "The substance of a Jew is the concern of the law". Indeed, in cases where the prohibition was not biblically ordained but only rabbinically introduced the Halachah manifested a tolerant attitude.[7]

Many halachic rulings were based on the consideration "So that the law may not be forgotten in Israel". The Rabbis held that it is right that a law be relaxed in order that the Torah and tradition be preserved in Israel.[8] An example is the ruling of the Talmudic Rabbis in regard to the observance of the Sabbath on a journey or in the wilderness if the actual day is not known. In cases where circumstances prevented a person from conforming to the law, the Rabbis applied a favourite dictum. He could be regarded "like a child held captive by Gentiles". He is the victim of an exceptional situation.

The tolerant attitude of the Rabbis is reflected in other rulings. The question was asked whether it would be right and proper to forbid the Cohanim to *duchan* in a community in which the majority of them desecrated the Sabbath in public, conduct which, according to the Halachah, disqualified them from performing this priestly function. It was, however, argued that this might

---

7   Ketuboth 60a; see M.S. Lew, The Jews of Poland pp. 31-2
8   Ketuboth 103b דלא משתכחה תורה מישראל

cause the Cohanim to disregard their priestly status and duties and thus become guilty of other serious sins. Indeed, they might marry women forbidden to them biblically and they might also defile themselves by coming into contact with the dead. They should rather be considered like "children held captive by Gentiles".[9]

The Rabbis' concern for certain sections of the community is evident from a Talmudic statement. Farmers and villagers came to the towns on market days which were held on Mondays and Thursdays. They came to sell their produce or to attend the law courts.[10] They would also take the opportunity to visit the House of Study.[11] The villagers were permitted to read the Megillah earlier than the 14th Adar – the day appointed for this reading – if that day happened to be the market day, so that they could be free to supply food and drink to their fellow-Jews in the cities.[12]

The Rabbis' love and regard for the land of Israel is shown by a sensitive attitude. They relaxed the rule which forbids a Jew to ask a non-Jew to perform work for him on the Sabbath that is scripturally forbidden to a Jew. However, if one bought a home or field in the Land of Israel he was permitted to ask a non-Jew to prepare a contract even on the Sabbath.[13]

A Scriptural verse[14] served as the basis of many halachic rulings. "Her ways are ways of pleasantness and all her paths are peace". The Sages believed that a central tenet of the Torah was to regulate the life of the people in

9 Shabbath 69b; J. Shabbath 7,1; Noam Vol 21, p. 303
10 Megillah, 1,2
11 Baba Kamma 82a
12 Rabbi Dr. J. Rabbinowitz, Mishnah Megillah, pp. 41-42
13 Gittin 8b and Tosefta ad loc.; Baba Kamma 80b
14 Proverbs 3,17

a spirit of peace and harmony. A remarkable Talmudic decision regarding levirate marriage[15] reflects the humanity of the Sages. Where levirate marriage was not acceptable to the parties concerned the procedure of *halitzah* permitted the widow to marry outside the family.[16]

The following is an informative and convincing example of the sympathy and beneficence of the Sages. If a man died and left a wife and child, and later the child died, the widow has no longer to marry her late husband's brother in accordance with the law of levirate marriage or to require the performance of *halitzah*. It was held that the words of the Torah indicated that only if there was no child at the time of the husband's death did the precept apply. Consequently, in the case under consideration, to subject her to a levirate marriage or *halitzah* after she had suffered a second loss would add to her grief. "Her ways are ways of pleasantness and all her paths are peace."[17]

The Scriptural verse alluded to is also quoted by the Rabbis in identifying the "four species" laid down in the Torah, which does not state what is meant by "boughs of the palm tree".[18] According to the rabbinic interpretation the phrase has reference to the *lulav*. "Whence do we know that 'branches of the palm tree' is to be indentified with the *lulav*? The answer is simple. 'Her ways are ways of pleasantness and all her paths are peace'." Rashi explains that it cannot refer to the plant that has thorns

15 Deuteronomy 25,5-10
16 Ibid.
17 Yebamoth 87b and Rashi ad loc.
18 Leviticus 23,40

for the Torah would not have enjoined to take such a plant to perform a *mitzvah*.[19]

The Talmud discusses the question of גרמא, indirect effect, on the Sabbath and Holy Days whereby certain acts, normally forbidden by the Halachah, would be permissible. If the individual does not himself perform the action but merely establishes a situation which causes the action to take place, then in certain instances this is permitted.[20] One example will serve: orthodox Jewish staff in hospitals may do certain work and use some instruments where גרמא only would be entailed.

The Mishnah gives the reason for many rules and regulations designed to foster and maintain peaceful relations between Jew and Gentile מפני דרכי שלום 'for the sake of peace'. It was the Rabbis' firm belief that the main objective of the law was to sustain peace and goodwill among all men. Thus we read: "Our Rabbis taught, Gentile poor should be provided for together with the Jewish poor..."[21]

R. Yose held that the rules laid down in the Mishnah on the ground of 'for the sake of peace' were legal obligations and could be enforced by the court.[22] Rashi was of the opinion that these rules were rabbinical enactments and not strict law, and moral rather than legal considerations motivated them. The furtherance of broad human cooperation and brotherhood[23] is, according to Maimonides, the purpose of the Rabbis' leniency.

---

19 Sukkah 32a
20 Shabbath 120b
21 Gittin 61a
22 Ibid. 59a-b
23 Baba Metzia 32b; Melachim 10,12

The economic level of the poorer classes was a matter disputed by the Rabbis. R. Akiba was of the opinion that the plot for a house, unless otherwise specified in the deed of sale, must not be less than four cubits by six (about seventy feet by ten and a half feet).[24] R. Ishmael differed firmly from this view. He insisted that such a site could be suitable for a stable rather than a house. It was R. Akiba's humanity and regard for the poor that may have influenced his decision. Thus some scholars held that no garden could be properly operated if it were less than half a kab (about 1500 square feet) in area. R. Akiba accepted a lower standard which would be the measure of the poorer classes. He further held that the smallest field must also have some part set aside for the poor.[25]

Concern for the poor lies no doubt behind a familiar Mishnaic ruling.[26] If a man dies leaving a small estate which becomes the subject of litigation between his heir, his wife and his creditor, R. Tarfon would solve the problem by "giving it to the one who is at the greatest disadvantage or by giving it to the weakest among them". R. Akiba dissented. He held that the court must not show pity in a civil suit. In his view such an attitude would be patronising and detract from the diginity of the poor.[27] An old tradition sheds light on the tender attitude of the Sages towards the deprived. "If you have taken a pledge from the poor", God says to the rich, "do not say he is your debtor and you are therefore justified in retaining his garment. Remember you are My debtor, your life is in My hand".[28]

24   M. Baba Bathra 6,4
25   Peah 3,6
26   Ibid.; Sifra on Kedoshim 2,5
27   M. Ketuboth 9,2
28   Exodus 22,24; Tanḥuma Mishpatim 9

A man must have regard for his servants and treat them with consideration. Servants who attended at table were to be offered of the same food eaten by the master.[29] Some scholars were accustomed to offer those waiting upon them at table of all the dishes served.[30] In their decisions and rulings the Rabbis were motivated by a deep concern and sympathy for fellowmen regardless of rank or station.

In Jewish teaching personal service includes hospitality. Both in the Bible and in the rabbinic literature we find an attitude to hospitality which is marked by a warmth of feeling. The narrative portions of Scripture and the traditions and tales recorded in the Talmud and Midrashim speak in praise of the practice of this virtue and testify to the high and prominent place accorded to hospitality in the Jewish scheme of living. Many halachic rulings relating to hospitality manifest an attitude on the part of the Sages which was clearly intended to encourage and promote this human practice. One example will suffice. The Rabbis permitted a would-be host to clear a barn or wine cellar on the Sabbath if it was necessary to do so in order to accommodate his guests. This task was normally disallowed on the Sabbath.[31] The relaxation of certain restrictions in order to enable a person to extend hospitality bears testimony to the Rabbis' profound regard for this social duty. The halachic principle of שעת הדחק, emergency, could be applied where hospitality was involved. The principle of הפסד מרובה, considerable loss, was taken account of in some of the Sabbath laws regarding the practice of hospitality.[32]

29 Maimonides, Abadim 9.8
30 Ketuboth 61b
31 Shabbath 126b; Maimonides, Shabbath 26,15; S.A.O.Ḥ. 333,1
32 S.A.Y.D. 68,11 Rema; Ibid. 69,6 Rema

In a survey of the attitude of the Sages to social duties and anti-social behaviour, the question of asceticism needs to receive attention. In the Torah there are two seemingly conflicting views. Concerning the Nazirite[33] we read, "Because his consecration unto God is upon his head". The hair of the Nazirite symbolised his dedication to God. Another verse reads[34] "And the priest shall prepare one for a sin offering and the other for a burnt offering and make atonement for him that he sinned by reason of the dead and he shall hallow his head that same day". Naḥmanides[35] comments: "He needs atonement when he returns to the enjoyment of mundane things". The expressions show a negative attitude towards abstinence.

The Nazirite was to make atonement for both his accidental defilement and for his vow to abstain from drinking wine, an unnecessary deprivation of a permitted pleasure. The surrender of that which is permitted leads to self-denial which the Sages did not favour.[36] Perhaps they discerned in such conduct an anti-social tendency which is alien to Judaism. The same contradictory views on asceticism are found in the Talmud.[37] Some utterances condemned abstinence.[38] What the Torah permits one should not regard as forbidden.[39]

Maimonides' attitude to the Nazir is ambivalent. In the Moreh Nebuchim[40] he speaks of the Nazir approvingly

33   Numbers 6,7
34   Ibid. 6,11
35   Naḥmanides on Numbers,6
36   J. Kiddushin 4,12
37   Taanith 11a
38   J. Nedarim 9,1
39   Ibid.
40   Guide III, 48

whereas in his Code he shows a negative approach.[41]

Isserls' comment is illuminating.[42] Referring to the sequence in the Torah of the section regarding the woman suspected of adultery and that concerning the Nazirite, he stresses the comment of the Sages that wine leads to immorality. The incident of the allegedly unfaithful wife should encourage people to become Nazirites and abstain from wine.

The Sages showed also great consideration and care for all living creatures. It is forbidden to inflict pain on animals. This prohibition lies behind several injunctions of the Torah.[43] In the Talmud[44] kindness to animals is at the basis of many of its rulings. The Rabbis enjoined that one must feed his animals first before he sits down to a meal. The ruling is based on the Biblical text[45]: "And I will give grass in the field for the cattle and thou shalt eat and be satisfied". The Rabbis noted that "cattle" is mentioned first. R. Ishmael used to feed his camel before he took food for himself. He no doubt remembered Proverbs[46]: "The righteous man regardeth the life of his beast". It is recorded[47] that R. Judah Hanasi suffered for ten years because he had failed to save a kid that tried to escape from slaughter.

Maimonides[48] explained the injunction which forbids the killing of an animal and its young on the same day as follows: "It is prohibited to slaughter an animal and its

41   Deoth 3,1
42   Numbers 5,11-31; 6,1-13; Nazir 2a; Torat Ha-Olah 3,71
43   Exodus 23,5; Deuteronomy 22,4
44   Baba Metzia 32a-b; Abodah Zarah 18b; Shabbath 128b S.A.O.H. 305,19
45   Deuteronomy 11,15
46   Proverbs 12,10
47   Baba Metzia 85a
48   Guide III, 48

young on the same day in order that people should be restrained and prevented from killing the two together in such a manner that the young is slain in the sight of the mother; for the pain of the animal under such circumstances is exceedingly great. There is no difference in this case between the pain of man and the pain of other living beings, since the love and tenderness of the mother for her young ones is not produced by reasoning but by feeling and this faculty exists not only in man, but in most living things". He says that the same reason underlies the prohibition in regard to the mother bird being taken with her young.[49]

The Rabbis were concerned that a Jew should do nothing that could offend the sensitivities of Gentiles and provoke their disapproval and criticism. Thus a non-Jewish contractor working for a Jew is not allowed to do so on the Sabbath. In the case of a Synagogue there is an additional reason for the prohibition. Gentiles do not permit work on their festivals in public and should Jews allow this to be done in their Synagogues it would cause a desecration of the Divine Name. It was equally held that if anything is forbidden to a Gentile but not to a Jew, especially in regard to food, a Jew must abstain from it.[50] Anything that is forbidden in Gentile places of worship cannot be permitted in the Synagogue for this would be a flagrant disregard of the sanctity of the Synagogue. Basing themselves on an erudite Responsum many rabbis would not allow smoking on weekdays in a Synagogue.[51]

The many rules and regulations that govern the

---

49   Deuteronomy 22,6ff
50   Rabbi A.I. Waldinberg, Responsa: Ziz Eliezer 5,3
51   Rabbi M. Feinstein, the distinguished contemporary Halachist, Responsa: Iggrot Mosheh O.H. 45

Synagogue reflect the sanctity and dignity accorded to it in the Halachah.[52] In the opinion of the Rabbis, without a Synagogue a community loses its sacred and strongest link with Judaism and Jewish life. Judaism and the community seem devalued. Religious and community life is weakened. The disappearance of a Synagogue may well cause Gentiles to point to Jewish religious indifference and laxity.[53]

It is clear that the principle "for the sake of peace", to which reference has been made, enabled the Jewish jurists to interpret various laws and to take a moderate view in cases where only a rabbinic prohibition was involved.[54] Furthermore, even in matters of Torah law the Rabbis sometimes felt justified in deciding on the ground that strict adherence to the law might cause איבה, hostility, ill-feeling.

The Halachah deemed it right to introduce rules that would provide for the Gentile poor even if such provision would deprive the Jewish needy. Maimonides holds that it was on the ground of this principle that the Rabbis permitted the introduction of certain ordinances and regulations. Many *Takkanoth* were rabbinically enacted and they derived their legal force from the acceptance of them by the communities.[55]

The Rabbis believed that the study of the Torah was not merely an intellectual pursuit but would lead to the good life, the life which embraced character and conduct, justice and righteousness.[56] Indeed, they declared that

52 Megillah 29a; Maimonides: Tefillah 11,1-23; S.A.O.H. 151
53 Rabbi M. Feinstein, Responsa: Iggrot Mosheh O.H. 45
54 Gittin 61a
55 Ibid; Baba Metzia 32b; Melachim 10,12; Hatam Sofer, Yoreh Deah 131
56 Kiddushin 40b

such study is even more acceptable to the All-present than burnt-offerings. For if a man studies Torah he knows the will of the All-present.[57] That knowledge was not the only objective of study of the law is implied in some of the rabbinic utterances. It was also an expression of religious enthusiasm and spiritual devotion. When one of the Sages, it is revealingly recorded, was engaged in study the atmosphere that surrounded him was ardent and glowing with intense spirituality. The atmosphere, says the Prince of Commentators, was generated by the Ministering Angels who assembled to hear from the Master's lips his exposition of the Law.[58]

Indeed the virtue of sympathy and consideration is implicit, as already mentioned, in the Jewish tradition and has influenced Jewish legislation. "The Torah begins and ends with an act of lovingkindness".[59] The Rabbis cite two incidents in support of their assertion. The beginning of the Torah tells that God clothed Adam and at the end of the Torah that He buried Moses.[60]

The importance of learning and education is stressed in Judaism. In the Halachah the status of scholars is clearly defined. They were accorded rights and privileges. They were exempt from certain taxes. Although witnesses were obliged to give their evidence standing, yet an exception could be made in the case of a learned man. Should he consider it beneath his dignity to give evidence at all, he could be exempted. This only applies to monetary cases. In criminal matters he would not be exempted.[61]

---

57   Aboth D'Rabbi Nathan, Soncino ed. Ch.4 p. 35
58   Sukkah 28a, Rashi ad loc.
59   Sotah 14a; cf. A. Marmorstein, Studies in Jewish Theology, p. 113
60   Genesis 3,21 and Deuteronomy 34,6
61   Maimonides: Eduth 1,2

The Rabbis emphasized the need of fellowship in study. It has been suggested that the fact that the Reading of the Torah, which has a two-fold purpose - study and prayer - was assigned to congregational worship stresses the same idea. Companionship in study would serve to encourage friendship among scholars.[62] Assiduous devotion to learned interests might lead to individualism.

Some scholars were as well-known for their regard and respect for each other as for their concern for fellowmen in general. Few could fail to admire them for their sensitivity and human sympathy.[63] The cruel persecutions and attacks on their people filled them with grief and distress.

The following incident reflects the deep feeling of R. Gamaliel. For several days his students noticed that when he entered the Academy his eyes were red from crying. On inquiry, they found that he was awakened each night by the moaning of a widow who was his next door neighbour. When he heard her groaning and crying he could not restrain his tears.[64]

That the Rabbis considered social contacts beneficial to the individual is evident from some halachic rulings. Indeed, according to Tosafoth[65], social isolation is a form of pain for man. A person, it was held, who was compelled to live a lonely existence because of personal embarrassment had the status of a sick person suffering from a non-dangerous illness. He would be allowed to have treatment on the Sabbath which entailed

62   Makkoth 10a
63   Aboth 4,15; 3,18
64   Sanhedrin 104,b
65   Shabbath 50b

infringement of restrictions that are only rabbinically prohibited.[66]

The sources show that some scholars were wholly devoted to the study of the Torah. Others, however, depended for their livelihood on a trade or business. A famous Rabbi[67] advised students and scholars not to interrupt other scholars in their studies during certain times of the year. Thus Rava urged his colleagues not to appear before him during the months of Nisan and Tishri. Nisan was the harvest period and Tishri the time of the vintage and olive pressing. He was clearly preoccupied during those months in outdoor business activities.

The poor economic conditions in which some scholars found themselves are described in the familiar rabbinic utterance: "Every day a Divine voice goes forth from Mount Ḥoreb and proclaims; 'The whole world is sustained for the sake of my son Ḥanina and Ḥanina, my son, has to subsist on a *kab* of carobs from one weekend to the next'."[68]

It is clear that some of the Talmudic Rabbis were engaged in farming.[69] "Get me a man to irrigate my field in my stead and I will act as a judge in your case." Generally speaking the scholars were known for their humility and piety. Only in a place where a scholar was unknown was he permitted to say: "I am a scholar", so that the people may show respect for his learning.[70]

Scholars were accorded esteem and consideration and

---

66   Ibid. 94b, Rashi ad loc.
67   Berakoth 35b
68   Ibid. 17b
69   Ketuboth 105a
70   Nedarim 62a

generally enjoyed trust and confidence.[71] The question was posed whether a scholar may transgress a light prohibition so that the ignorant may not offend against a serious transgression.[72]

Early in this chapter I considered the concept of הוראת שעה "a decision of the hour". Indeed, it was a radical measure for the preservation of the Torah in emergency conditions. Maimonides writes: "If the Sages perceived that the times demanded the abolition of certain positive commandments or the need for transgressing some negative commandments in order to bring the people back to Judaism or to save many Jews from transgressing other observances, they were permitted to do what "the need of the hour" demanded. Just as a surgeon amputates a patient's hand or foot so that he may live and be well, similarly the court may, when the hour demanded, permit the violation of certain commandments so that the other precepts may be preserved." This is in harmony, he says, with the Talmudic principle: 'a man may desecrate one Sabbath for a dangerously sick person so that the patient may be enabled to observe many Sabbaths in the future.'[73]

Conversely, the sources refer to instances in which heavy penalties were imposed upon offenders even when the law of the Torah did not lay down such severe penalties. The Sages ruled that in such cases "the need of the hour" demanded harsh measures.[74]

There was a tradition that under certain conditions it

71 Ibid. 62b
72 Erubin 32b
73 Mamrim 2,4; Yoma 85b אמרה תורה חלל עליו שבת אחת כדי שישמר שבתות הרבה
74 Sanhedrin 46a

was the prerogative, and even the duty, of the court to inflict heavy penalties "which are not in accordance with the Halachah."[75] Maimonides held that the power of the court to inflict penalties unauthorized by the Torah was founded on the principle of erecting a fence around the law lest the people disregard the law. But such measures were only temporary. They were not accorded the binding force of the law.[76]

The purpose of emergency decisions was clearly to preserve the laws of the Torah and the religious and moral discipline of the community. It is safe to say that notwithstanding the extensive powers granted to the courts they only exercised these in exceptional situations.

Indeed, the Rabbis endeavoured to teach and guide the life of the people by precept and example. Their perceptive insight and inspiration sustained their desire and determination to uphold the law as a living force, perennially relevant and refreshing, ensuring its unity, integrity and stability.

75   J. Ḥagigah 78a and Yebamoth 90b
76   Sanhedrin 24,4; Makkoth 1,6

CHAPTER EIGHT

RETURN AND REHABILITATION

The humanity of the Halachah was extended to the criminal, the sinner and the fallen in the community. The Sages looked upon crime as a sin, the punishment for which was not always to be meted out by fellow humans. While they believed in the inherent goodness and dignity of man, they realized that there were those whose conduct, often due to circumstances, fell below the minimum standards. The court had to decide in each individual case as to the appropriate punishment and its enforcement.

As already mentioned, the sources, apart from the two cases recorded in the Torah,[1] rarely refer to imprisonment or length of sentences other than in capital cases. The absence of such information would suggest that imprisonment was but infrequently imposed.

As the main purpose of punishment was, in the opinion of the Rabbis, in order to reform the character of the offender, they believed monetary compensation to be a more effective punishment in many cases.

---

1 Leviticus 24, 10ff and Numbers 15,32ff.

Theft and robbery are both serious crimes yet a distinction was drawn between them in the Torah. While the thief steals secretly the robber takes things openly and even by force. Both are obliged to restore the stolen goods or make monetary or *in specie* restitution. For there is in Jewish law a civil aspect to both offences. The robber was to restore the articles taken or their value whereas the thief for stealing chattels was to pay double and for stealing, selling or slaughtering an ox or a sheep the penalty was four or fivefold. Theft was considered the more serious crime, declares a Talmudic Rabbi, because by his furtive action the thief showed fear of human punishment but not of the judgment of God. The robber denied both an individual's right as well as the sovereignty of God.[2]

Other systems of law, in contrast, regarded robbery the more serious offence, often punishable by death. Indeed, robbery was deemed a grave crime against the state whose authority the robber openly and flagrantly defied. Hence he was a public enemy.

One of the fundamental doctrines of Judaism reflected in the Halachah is that the sinner can return and repent and thus feel relieved of his burden of guilt. In the words of Isaiah[3] "that the wicked forsake his way and the man of iniquity his thoughts, and let him return unto the Lord and He will have mercy upon him".

Through the act of repentance man is able to reform and rehabilitate himself. To help him in his efforts to repent the Rabbis ruled that a man who stole timber and used it in the construction of a building was not required to demolish the building in order to restore the timber to

2   Exodus 22,3; Ibid 21,37; Leviticus 5,23; Baba Kamma 79b
3   Isaiah 55,7

the owner. While according to the strict law[4] the offender was to return the article stolen even if it involved the demolition of the building, the Rabbis permitted monetary restitution.

The enactment of the Sages was designed to help offenders to a new start of honest and moral conduct.[5] It was feared that many, unless shown sympathy by the law, would reach the point of no return. The two famous Schools, Beth Shammai and Beth Hillel, differed fundamentally in this matter.[6]

The Sages showed a remarkable concern and solicitude for the misguided, the erring and the fallen. The Mishnah emphasized this humane attitude. "The monies restored by robbers and usurers should not be accepted by the owners, and an owner who does accept them incurs the disfavour of the Sages".[7] According to R. Johanan this Mishnah can be traced back to the days of R. Judah Hanasi and no doubt had its origin in the following incident:[8] A robber once felt moved to repent and make amends for his misdeeds. Thereupon his wife said to him: "*Raka* (you fool) if you will do as you feel, then even your girdle will not remain yours". The plea of the wife had its effect. It dissuaded him from making amends. The Mishnah in question according to Tosafoth, too, was taught in the days of R. Judah Hanasi "neither before his time nor after". Hence he instituted the ruling for his own generation only because of the particular incident and not for future generations.

4   Leviticus 5,23
5   S.A.Ḥ.M. 360,1
6   Gittin 55a
7   Eduyoth 7,9; Baba Kamma 66b
8   Baba Kamma 94b; A. Büchler, Studies in Sin and Atonement pp. 387 and 394

It was indeed a bold enactment that freed robbers and those who lent on interest from legal responsibility. Some Rabbinic authorities of a later period were surprised at its introduction. However, many were guilty of these evil practices, and measures had to be introduced to arrest the trend. If offenders were compelled to restore the stolen goods or the interest charges, the financial burden would be too heavy for them to bear. In order to help them to reform the Rabbis ruled that even if they were prepared to make adequate compensation it should not be accepted from them. The purpose of punishment was to diminish sin in society. It was feared that the need for restitution in such cases might discourage those who wished to start life again on the right road.[9]

There were some Rabbis who held that this Talmudic ordinance[10] could be radical in effect and was against public policy. While it was an encouragement to some offenders who sincerely sought the way to reformation it could increase robbery in society. Hence some Sages maintained that it was intended for that particular generation only when it was most essential.[11] The balance of opinion was that the offender, who was genuinely seeking to make good, had to be assisted in his desire to take his place again in the community. Others thought that the ordinance might prove harmful and they surrounded it with restrictions and limitations. In their view it was not to be applied to the habitual offender.

Yet despite the lenient enactment there remained a moral obligation which by the standard of the Higher Court (the Heavenly Court) obliged the offenders to

9   Baba Kamma 94b
10   Ibid.
11   Ibid. Tosafoth ad loc

make restitution which would be enforced by the courts. However, that Rabbi Judah Hanasi felt constrained to introduce an ordinance, which was contrary to the Biblical law[12], shows how concerned he was to encourage delinquents to repent. Clearly, the enactment applied generally and not to those only who expressed a desire to return to an honest life.

Another example reflects the sympathy and concern of the Sages. The Ordeal of the wife suspected of infidelity is enjoined in the Torah.[13] But according to the Mishnah[14] R. Johanan b. Zakkai abolished the rite soon after the destruction of the Temple. His decision was clearly motivated by the conditions of the times, when the national catastrophe engendered low moral standards. Many men, perhaps permissive themselves, could hardly be allowed to bring charges against their wives on the ground of their misconduct. This view mentioned by Rabbi Yomtov Lipmann Heller (1579-1654)[15] does not fully explain R. Johanan's daring decision. The Talmud however finds support for R. Johanan's ruling in the words of the Torah[16] "And the man shall be clear from iniquity and the woman shall bear her iniquity". On the basis of the words "and the man shall be clear" the Rabbis explained that if the husband was not blameless in his moral behaviour, the Ordeal would prove ineffective. R. Johanan considered that the Ordeal as a legal and moral procedure was to be abolished.

With the Golden Rule in mind, "And thou shalt love thy neighbour as thyself", the Rabbis enjoined that an

---

12 Leviticus 5,23
13 Numbers 5,11-31
14 Sotah 9,9
15 Tosafoth Yom Tov on Sotah 9,9
16 Numbers 5,31

easy death be chosen for those condemned, that is one of speed and causing as little humiliation as possible.[17] For the sentence was to be carried out with compassion. According to the Torah the body of the executed was to receive reverent treatment and was to be buried without delay.[18] Death, in Jewish teaching, is an expiation for sin and concern for the dignity of the human personality must be shown even to the criminal. Man is created in the Divine image and, in the language of the Rabbis, it is an outrage to disfigure and desecrate the image of God. The Rabbis considered murder a crime of the gravest enormity. Maimonides[19] held that murder, more than any other crime, leads to the destruction of civilization. Yet, despite the sinfulness of murder the Sages' attitude to capital punishment was such that they virtually abolished it. Indeed, some held that no human being should condemn another to death.

Concern for human life lies also behind the ruling of Maimonides regarding the informer.[20] Talmudic law looked upon informers as pariahs, because their sinister activities endangered Jewish life and property. It laid down rigorous measures in regard to them. Maimonides, however, ruled that these measures were to be applied only whilst the informer was in the course of carrying out his evil design.[21] Maimonides' humanity reached out to all. He urged judges to be particularly careful to treat delinquents with respect and sympathy. On the phrase[22] "Israel hath sinned", R. Abba b. Zabda commented[23]

17 Sanhedrin 45a
18 Deuteronomy 21;22,23
19 Rotzeaḥ 4,9 השחתת יישובו של עולם
20 Ḥobel U-Mazik 8,9
21 Ibid.
22 Joshua 7,11
23 Sanhedrin 44a; Edels ad loc.

"Even though the people have sinned they are still called 'Israel'." He compared the sinners in Israel to the myrtle which though it grows among thorns is still a myrtle. Edels comments significantly. "Even though a Jew has sinned and transgressed the entire law he is deemed a Jew in all respects."

Ezra included in the Second Return all types of Jews; those who had married foreign women, who had desecrated the Sabbath as well as those who had forgotten Hebrew.[24] He was motivated by his belief that, in the ancestral home and among their own people, the weak and estranged would return and adhere to the teachings of their faith.

That this attitude was justified was shown when the descendants of those who returned from the Babylonian captivity demonstrated their faith and showed obedience to the practices and traditions of Judaism. In contrast, Moses, Elijah and Isaiah were rebuked by God for condemning Israel.[25]

The Hebrew prophets called sinners to repentance, assuring them of its efficacy.[26] The story of R. Meir and Beruriah is well-known. When certain evil persons caused her husband pain and distress he prayed for their death. She disapproved of his action interpreting the words of the Psalmist as expressing God's desire for the destruction of sin and not of sinners. She urged him to pray, rather, that they repent of their evil ways.[27]

Maimonides ruled that we must show kindness and consideration to sinners who believe in the fundamentals

24   Ezra 10,1-5
25   Yalkut Shimeoni on Isaiah 6, 406
26   Isaiah 55,6-7; Jeremiah 3,14,22; Hosea 6,1;4,2; Malachi 3,7
27   Psalm 104,35; Berakoth 10a

of Judaism.[28] He also ruled[29] that the lives of both the righteous and of the sinners alike must be saved when threatened with danger.

In Judaism any lapse, however grave, can be atoned for by sincere repentance, remorse and reparation.[30] The belief in the integrating power of repentance is a doctrine stressed in Jewish thought.[31] Before God created the world, say the Sages, He created repentance for man.[32]

As already mentioned, in the opinion of the Jewish jurists, the purpose of punishment was to improve the offender.Where there could be no pardon, punishment was to be imposed but even then it was not to be devoid of mercy. Indeed, punishment was neither designed to inflict torment upon the offender nor to humiliate him. Human dignity must be respected even in a criminal.[33] "Even an utterly wicked man throughout his life", said R.Simeon b. Yoḥai, "if he repents we must not remind him of his former evil conduct," as it is said, "As for the wickedness of the wicked, he shall not fall thereby in the day that he turneth from his wickedness!"[34] He believed with the Prophet that an individual's past life and conduct do not, in God's judgment, determine the future and that the truly repentant will not suffer for his former behaviour. While the repentance of the criminal was not always proof of complete reform, in thought and in deed, his penitence was to be encouraged.

The remarkable concern of the Rabbis for the erring

28   Rotzeaḥ 13,14
29   Ibid.
30   Ezekiel 18,23; Kiddushin 40b
31   Pesaḥim 119a; Rosh Hashanah 17b; Sanhedrin 103a; Yoma 86a-b
32   Pesaḥim 54a; Genesis Rabbah 50,52
33   Deuteronomy 25,1-3
34   Ezekiel 33,12; Kiddushin 40b and Tosefta ad loc.

and sinful finds its climax in the bold Talmudic dictum
יִשְׂרָאֵל, אַף עַל פִּי שֶׁחָטָא יִשְׂרָאֵל הוּא, a Jew who has
sinned against his faith and people is still a Jew.[35] Though
expressed in aggadic language and style, it reflects an
halachic concept consistent with the legal and theological
thinking of the Sages who often clothed halachic
doctrines and principles in concise and arresting
midrashic phrase.[36]

The status of the מוּמָר, an apostate Jew, in regard to
marriage, divorce, *halitzah* and *yibum* and in the laws
relating to inheritance and burial, supports the view
expressed. It lays emphasis on the strong bonds that bind
a Jew to his people and religion. More often than not, the
sinful and apostate Jew remains loyal in his heart to his
roots. He may well have repented of his sin and apostasy.
Through his sincere return and fidelity he may have been
restored spiritually and conscientiously to his ancestral
faith and thus may have regained his Jewish moral
awareness. To deprive him of his birthright, status and
identity would be tantamount to a denial of his rights and
his inner yearning for God and a desire for communion
with his fellow-Jews.[37]

That this rabbinic doctrine, often regarded as aggadic,
has served as a basic legal maxim reveals the depth,
insight and humanity of the Halachah.

---

35 Sanhedrin 44a
36 Professor M. Elon, Hamishpat ha-Ivri vol. 1 p.145
37 S.A.Y.D. 268,12 Rema. A מוּמָר who reverts to Judaism requires,
    according to some authorities, a special ritual when he undertakes to
    observe in the future the laws of Judaism. Some Halachists also insist on
    ritual immersion in a Mikveh as in the case of proselytes.

CHAPTER NINE

THE GENERAL WELFARE

The deep concern of the Jewish jurists for the welfare of all classes regardless of position or station, the humanitarian rules relating to the weak and fallen, the deprived and oppressed in society, their consideration for animals and birds, helped to influence Western legislators and social reformers. Thus it is widely maintained that the isolation of lepers in medieval Europe as well as other measures in the public interest were clearly based on Jewish law, Biblical and rabbinic, designed to protect society.[1]

The clear difference in Jewish law between the private domain and the public domain is evidence of the Rabbis' insistence on man's duty to protect himself as well as the well-being of his fellowmen, showing respect for other persons, their property, safety and general welfare.

Implicit in the Biblical injunction[2] "Thou shalt not destroy" is that a man's life is sacred and is not his own. He must do everything that will ensure his health and

1   Professor N. Isaacs: The Legacy of Israel p. 383
2   Deuteronomy 20.19

well-being.[3] It has been aptly said that if a man is indifferent to his own welfare he is unlikely to be concerned about the welfare of his fellow men. The idea is clearly enshrined in the precept "Thou shalt love thy neighbour as thyself."[4]

Whosoever endangers his life, the Rabbis declared, violates a positive precept of the Torah.[5] Maimonides, in re-affirming this principle says, "If one states: I want to endanger my life, what concern is it of others, disciplinary flogging is to be inflicted on him".[6] For no man can claim that his physical welfare is his own concern alone. Man is not the owner of his life or body. Any act which endangers his life is a transgression against the will of God. Man's life was entrusted to him by God to guard it well.

A Biblical injunction which was clearly intended to serve as a general principle for the protection of human life and health, is to be found in the verse. "When thou buildest a new house, then thou shalt make a parapet for thy roof that thou bring not blood upon thy house, if any man fall from thence."[7]   Houses in Eastern countries had flat roofs which were used for domestic and social purposes, including eating and sleeping and for receiving guests. It was obligatory to erect a fence around them to prevent accidents. Failure to protect human life exposes the occupier to liability and guilt. The Rabbis extended this prohibition to include many cases where danger to life exists through negligence. If one rents a house he is in

3   Shabbath 140b
4   Leviticus 19,18
5   Deuteronomy 4,9
6   Rotzeah, 11,5
7   Deuteronomy 22,8

duty bound to provide adequate protection. Failure to do so rendered him liable for damage caused.

The Sages explained the reason for the precept. "Any place, not only a house, where there is danger that one may fall requires a fence, including pits, caves, trenches and ditches."[8] The Talmud understands the injunction to include everything that can endanger a man's life.[9] "A man should not breed a dog unless he is kept on a chain."[10] The Codes[11] prescribe the general rule:"It is a positive commandment to remove any stumbling block that may endanger life." For it says: "Take heed and guard your life."[12] If one did not remove the stumbling-blocks and left them so that they could cause danger, one had transgressed the injunction "Thou shalt not put blood in thy house."[13]

The Rabbis also ruled that a community, like an individual, has a duty to remove from public places anything that may cause danger to pedestrians and travellers. Accordingly, while normal work was not permitted on *Hol Hamoed* public services were allowed to be maintained.[14] It was clearly the duty of the civic authorities to provide for the protection and safety of the life and health of the inhabitants, to maintain the public roads and to provide street lights in order to prevent serious accidents.

To protect the health of the people a Mishnaic ruling did not permit carcasses, graves and tanneries to remain

8 Sifre Ki Teze 65
9 Ketuboth 41b
10 Baba Kamma 83a
11 Maimonides: Rotzeah 11,1-11 S.A.H.M. 427,8
12 Deuteronomy 4,9
13 Deuteronomy 22,8
14 Moed Katan 5a

within an area of fifty cubits from the town.[15] A permanent threshing floor may not be made within fifty cubits from the city.[16] Rashi's comment is significant. "On account of the chaff that flies about which may be injurious to health". Anything that caused danger to health or affected the beauty or cleanliness of a city, the Council was permitted to remove or destroy regardless of the loss to the owner. The amenities of the town had to be preserved.[17] "Trees may not be grown within a distance of twenty five cubits from a city or fifty cubits if they are carob or sycamore or eucalyptus".[18] Abba Saul says: "Any tree that bears no fruit may not be grown within a distance of fifteen cubits".[19] If the city was there first the tree should be cut down and no compensation paid. If the tree was there first, it should be cut down and compensation paid. If it was uncertain which was there first, the tree should be cut down and there was no liability for compensation. These regulations were introduced, according to Rashi, in order to preserve the beauty of the town.

The needs of the city included, as already mentioned, proper roads and streets as well as valid *Mikvaoth*, (ritual immersion baths).[20] After the winter rains it was necessary to repair the roads for the Passover pilgrims.

Since the drinking of water could prove a danger to health, the Rabbis ruled[21] "One should not drink water either from river pools direct with the mouth or (by

15   Baba Bathra 25a
16   Ibid. 24b
17   Baba Metzia 117a
18   M. Baba Bathra 2,7
19   Ibid.
20   Shekalim 1,1
21   Abodah Zarah 12b

drawing of water) with the one hand without examining it; if he drinks it his blood shall be upon his head for it is dangerous." Accordingly, it devolved upon the authorities of the city to arrange for a supply of proper drinking water.

The watering of animals was permitted, under certain conditions, on the Sabbath in order to preserve their life and health.[22] It was a duty to erect upright boards around the wells.[23] An area around them being enclosed by a square, even slightly defined, rendered them a private domain which permitted their use for cattle on the Sabbath. The Talmud also lays down rules respecting fountains in the towns.[24]

In ancient times, roads mainly served for travel and for transportation to the markets. Later, they were also used for military purposes, for the movement of troops and provisions. King Solomon who had chariots for his personal use as well as for trade must have given attention to road building.[25]

Isaiah[26] makes reference to levelling of roads; he also speaks of removing stones from the highway so that the returning exiles meet with no obstacles on the road.[27] A tax for keeping roads in repair in Persian times is mentioned in the Bible.[28] The importance of roads was thus early recognized.[29]

There are rules laid down in the Halachah regarding

---

22   M. Erubin 2,1
23   Ibid.
24   Baba Metzia 108a
25   1 Kings 10,26
26   Isaiah 42,16
27   Ibid. 57,14 and 62,10
28   Ezra 4,13-20; 7,24
29   Psalm 107; Lamentations 1,4 The roads leading to Jerusalem were usually crowded with pilgrims but are now desolate, in mourning.

the width of different roads. "A private path must be four cubits wide, a road connecting two towns (used exclusively by the people of the two towns) eight cubits wide". A public road must have sixteen cubits in width. The roads leading to a City of Refuge, as mentioned before, must be thirty-two cubits wide."[30]

These rules were doubtless to maintain a free flow of traffic and to ensure road safety. The prescribed widths of roads required by Jewish law depended on the volume of traffic.[31] Even the private road was to be wide enough to allow two carts coming from opposite directions to pass without delay.[32]

The Mishnah[33] makes reference to public needs that were met by the annual contribution of *shekalim.* The majority of the commentators explain the Mishnah as dealing with the provision of facilities for the pilgrims or for fugitives fleeing to a City of Refuge. It can also be explained that it applied generally as the duty to maintain the roads in good repair for the benefit of the public.

The Halachah[34] prescribed both height and width beneath a tree that stretched into the public domain. As to height enough had to be cut away to allow "a camel and its rider to pass by." Regarding the width it was required that a camel laden with bundles of branches could pass by comfortably. These provisions were clearly laid down in the public interest. It was also held that overhanging branches of all trees should be cut away close to the street in order to guard against טומאה, Levitical uncleanness.

30 Baba Bathra 100 a-b
31 Ibid. See Rashbam ad loc
32 Ibid.
33 Shekalim 1,1
34 Baba Bathra 27b

Similarly, among the ten special regulations applied to Jerusalem was one that forbade projecting beams or balconies from houses. As in the case of overhanging branches two different reasons have been suggested. It was because of the fear of טומאה, defilement, that might be conveyed to passers by or travellers seeking rest and shelter beneath them. Prevention of accidents was the other reason for this regulation. Indeed, in the case of Jerusalem it was a precautionary measure in the interests of the pilgrims whose knowledge of the city and its streets was but scant.[35]

The duty to preserve the environment is emphasized in the following passage. "The pious men of former generations used to hide their thorns and broken glass in their fields at a depth of three handbreadths below the surface so that even the plough might not be hindered by them".[36] Hillel's Golden Rule served as a general principle.[37] For the damage caused can affect an individual and the public. The Rabbis introduced ordinances against causing damage to the environment which could endanger the safety and detract from the aesthetic enjoyment of the public at large.

The regulations against the killing of animals, the destruction of plants and pollution of the air were laid down for the same reason.[38]

The destruction of trees or the devastation of the land was forbidden. The trees of a besieged city might not be cut down because they were vital to man.[39] The Rabbis in extending the warning against the destruction of

35 Baba Kamma 82b; Rashi ad loc; Oholoth 1,2
36 Baba Kamma 30a
37 Shabbath 31b
38 Maimonides; Shechenim 11,1-4
39 Deuteronomy 20,19

anything that is useful found support for their opinion in the same verse.

The Biblical words,[40] "To dress it and to keep it" refer to the garden which God had planted. They are at the basis of a number of laws and regulations designed to protect the environment. To adhere scrupulously to these regulations was both a legal and moral duty.[41]

The Rabbis were particularly concerned about the preservation of the beauty of the Land of Israel and the provision of amenities for its citizens. The mountains that surrounded Jerusalem and its remarkable elevation imparted a special beauty to it. "Of the ten measures of beauty that came down to the world, Jerusalem took nine".[42]

An old tradition relates that David and Samuel were in Ramah engaged in the embellishment of the world and consulting about building the Temple. Rashi understands the word נויות as referring to an academy of learning and instruction. Some commentators take the word to indicate a college or place of residence, referring to the dwellings of the sons of the prophets whom Samuel attracted to himself in Ramah. But the word may also be understood literally connoting beauty.[43]

The Mishnah disapproves the rearing of small cattle in the Land of Israel. They are apt to stray into other persons' fields and cause damage. Rashi adds that they may affect adversely the cultivation and settlement in Eretz Yisrael which Jews are bound in duty to maintain.[44]

---

40 Genesis 2,15
41 Maimonides: Shechenim 10,1-5
42 Kiddushin 49b עשרה קבים יופי ירדו לעולם תשעה נטלה ירושלים
43 Zebaḥim 54,b; cf 1 Samuel 19,18; 2 Kings 6,1
44 Baba Kamma 79b; Rashi ad loc: משום ישוב ארץ ישראל; Pesaḥim 50b

As already indicated if a man was about to buy a house in Eretz Yisrael he was allowed to instruct a Gentile to prepare a deed of sale on the Sabbath. The reason is clear. To reside in the Land of Israel is a religious duty.[45] Tosafoth explain that this lenient attitude of the Sages applies only to acquiring property in the Land of Israel but not in the case of other precepts. The settlement of Jews in the Land of Israel was of permanent benefit to the entire Jewish people.[46] The ruling that an appropriate benediction is to be recited on beholding inhabited and developed cities in Eretz Yisrael points to its sacred character and is in harmony with the Rabbis' love for the land. Equally, on seeing destroyed and desolate cities the acknowledgment of the Divine hand is to be accompanied by a blessing as an expression of melancholy sentiment.[47]

Consideration for the beauty of Jerusalem and care for its environs was of special concern to the Rabbis.[48] Various restrictions are mentioned in the sources which were clearly intended to protect the city against anything vulgar and unseemly. Tanneries, chicken runs and beehives had to be situated at a certain distance from the city.[49] According to a Talmudic ruling no one was allowed to enter the Temple Mount with shoes or dust on his feet, with his staff or with his wallet.[50] This was no doubt in order to show respect and to maintain the cleanliness of the site.[51] The streets of Jerusalem were swept daily.[52]

---

45   Gittin 8b; Baba Kamma 80b
46   Ibid. Tosafoth
47   Berakoth 58b
48   Kiddushin 49b
49   M. Baba Bathra 2,9
50   Berakoth 54a
51   Ibid.
52   Baba Metzia 26a

It is of interest that even in Temple times no additions were allowed to be made to the city without consulting the King, a prophet, the Urim and Thummim or the Sanhedrin.[53] It would seem from the foregoing that the Halachah showed concern for the environment and provided measures for its protection. This interest in ecology is not only a desideratum of modern times.

The Rabbis' regard for the general welfare of the community is evident from their attitude to price controls. They refer to the Scriptural requirements. "And when the days of her purification are fulfilled, for a son or for a daughter, she shall bring a lamb of the first year for a burnt-offering, and a young pigeon; or a turtle-dove for a sin offering unto the door of the tent of meeting, unto the priest".[54] Generally, such offerings after confinement and purification were brought by the women at the Festivals when they went up to Jerusalem. Owing to distance or other difficulties they were allowed to do so at longer intervals and offer up many "pairs of doves or pigeons of the first year".

It happened at a certain time that the price of a pair of doves in Jerusalem had risen to a golden denar (twenty five silver denars). Rabban Simeon b. Gamaliel said. "By this Temple, I will not allow the night to pass by before they cost but a (silver) denar". He went into the court and ruled: "If a woman suffered five definite miscarriages or five issues, she need bring but one offering, and she may then eat of the sacrifices and she is not bound to offer the other sacrifices (for the other four mishaps). And that very day the price of a pair of doves stood at a quarter of silver denar each."[55]

53 M. Shebuoth 2,2; M. Sanhedrin 1,5
54 Leviticus 12,6
55 M. Keritoth 1,7

Another incident recorded in the Talmud[56] sheds lights upon the strenuous efforts of the Sages to control prices. The eminent Mar Samuel was among the Rabbis who opposed monopolies and the raising of prices of commodities and utensils. In his opinion while the principles of the Halachah were fundamental and immutable, the Halachah responded to changed human needs under new economic and social conditions.

The Torah forbids leaven on Passover. The Rabbis extended the prohibition to utensils that have absorbed leaven. With regard to earthenware vessels, Rab ruled that such vessels should be broken and discarded. Dealers in earthenware saw an opportunity to charge high prices for new vessels which were in great demand before the Passover Festival. Samuel ruled that these utensils need not be broken but could be made fit for use after the Passover. He urged the merchants of earthenware to sell cheaply. If they raised the price, he warned them, he would permit the use of the pots that had absorbed leaven after Passover.[57]

The Rabbis regarded the raising of prices above their actual value as a serious threat to the economic welfare of the public.They explained that the Psalmist's prayer "Break the arm of the wicked"[58] had reference to those who raised prices and thereby oppressed the poor.[59] Accordingly, to prevent such activities the court had a duty to appoint officers whose task it was to control prices[60] and who could impose monetary fines and stripes

56   Pesaḥim 30a.
57   Ibid.
58   Psalm 10,15
59   Megillah 17b
60   Baba Bathra 89a; Maimonides: Mechirah 14,1

upon offenders. Wholesalers of foods were only to have a small profit while retailers were allowed a larger margin.[61] Similarly, the Talmud forbids agencies or middlemen to deal in articles of food. The farmer was to sell direct to the consumer.[62]

Maimonides ruled:[63] "It is forbidden to do business in commodities - the necessities of life - in the Land of Israel." It is obvious that these rules were designed to control prices which would otherwise be higher and bear harshly upon the poor. Hence, if a certain article of food was in plenty and there was no risk that the middlemen might cause the price to soar there would be no need to control the sale of such articles. Thus where oil was in abundance the activities of middlemen would not be forbidden. In any event care was taken to prevent unscrupulous merchants from taking advantage of the poor.[64]

The question of export and import, with their effects upon prices and the attendant economic conditions, was the concern of the religious leaders. A Talmudic rule did not permit merchants to export from the Land of Israel fruits, foods, wine, oil and fine flour. R. Judah permitted the export of wine because it would help to reduce impropriety and permissiveness in the Holy Land.[65]

The Halachah did not countenance the export of treasures which had a historical or scientific significance and enriched the spiritual and cultural life of the country. The Jerusalem Talmud disapproved of books and Scrolls

---

61 S.A.Ḥ.M. 231,20
62 Baba Bathra 91a, Rashi ad loc.
63 Mechirah 14,2
64 Baba Bathra 91a
65 Ibid.

of the Law in the Holy Land being taken out of it.[66] Hence, rare manuscripts and art treasures would not be allowed to be exported, for such treasures enhanced the prestige, honour, culture and reputation of a country.

The sources show that the Rabbis introduced ordinances designed to spare the feelings of the poor. Contrasted with the affluence of the rich certain situations would cause the poor embarrassment.[67] Indeed, the Talmud records many decrees that were introduced out of regard for the sentiments of the poor.[68] The Sages also warned people not to live beyond their means.[69] The poor were not permitted to offer the sacrifices prescribed for the rich seeing that the Torah required different sacrifices from the prosperous and the poor. The economic circumstances of each class were taken into account. The poor were not to undertake burdens which they could not afford. Parents were not to incur expenditure too heavy to bear even in order to provide a wedding banquet for a child. Similarly, the rich were to refrain from flaunting their wealth lest they embarrass the poor in their midst.

The Sages frowned upon all class distinction and ostentation. Jacob warned his sons as they were about to visit Egypt against doing anything that might arouse jealousy and envy.[70]

Among the tasks of the Seven Elders appointed by communities was the duty to introduce measures against luxury and overspending by individuals. Indeed, it is

---

66   Sanhedrin 3,9 and Commentaries
67   Taanith 8,1 and Pesaḥim 82a
68   Moed Katan 27a-b
69   Sefer Ha-Ḥinuch 123
70   Genesis 42,1; Genesis Rabbah 91,6

enlightening to note the sympathy and care for the less prosperous.[71]

The sumptuary laws adopted in the Middle Ages were designed to ensure that family festivities were modest and unostentatious. The number of guests to be invited was limited by the communal leaders and subject to the requirements of a particular function. The leaders of the people were always to show an example to others. R. Gamaliel set such an example and he was honoured for it.[72]

While the Rabbis showed a deep regard for learning and instruction and accorded high honour and dignity to scholars, they equally showed concern for the unlearned. In a spirit of true humanity they manifested sympathy for the sensitivities of the uninformed whose embarrassment they sought to avoid.

The ceremony of the bringing of the First Fruits[73] was to be accompanied by a declaration to be recited in Hebrew.[74] Those who could not do so in Hebrew had to repeat it after the officiating priest. To avoid discrimination against the ignorant, the Rabbis ordained that learned and unlearned were to repeat the words of the declaration after the priest. "Beforetime all that could recite the prescribed Declaration recited it; and all that could not recite it repeated it (after the Priest) but when these refrained (out of shame) from bringing their First Fruits, it was ordained that both those who could recite it and those that could not should repeat the declaration (the words) after the Priest".[75]

71 Baba Bathra 10a
72 Moed Katan 27a-b
73 Deuteronomy 26,1-11
74 Ibid.
75 M. Bikkurim 3,7

Regard for the unlearned is to be found in the liturgical changes with respect to the public Reading of the Law. Originally the person who was called to the Reading of the Law read his portion. In later times, in order not to put anyone to shame or to deprive the untutored from being called up, the weekly Torah portion would be read by a person practised and proficient.

From early times the Jewish jurists thought it right to introduce ordinances and enactments in the public interest. Such enactments were designed to serve a two-fold purpose: to pay due regard to public policy and to safeguard individuals' well-being. To preserve the integrity and health of the community was another objective. In some cases such enactments combined law and equity. One or two examples out of many will suffice. The commandment "Thou shalt not steal" has a wider meaning than theft and robbery. A person's property is his sacred possession and Jewish law forbids any form of acquisition of such property by unlawful means. Mis-representation, cheating and taking unfair advantage are equally forbidden. Indeed, all dealings in which a person acts against the rights and interests of his neighbour come within the notions of theft and robbery. The ownership of an individual must not be usurped or affected. In the case of conflict between the communal interests and those of an individual, the rights of the former take precedence.

The enactments of the Rabbis and of later halachic luminaries served to preserve the continuity of Jewish law and its creative development. As has been said earlier, the Rabbis' concern for the welfare of the community and society in no way diminished their profound regard for the personality, intrinsic worth and rights of the individual. They believed that the individual owed duties to the community and group of which he was a member, even as the community and society depended on his loyalty and participation in its beneficent and wide-ranging endeavours for the general welfare. Indeed, nothing human was deemed beyond their combined ken and collective responsibility.

No more fitting close to this brief outline suggests itself than a word of praise and recognition of the contribution of the leading authorities, rabbinic and lay, who throughout the ages, amidst storm and sunshine, frustration and freedom, continued to inspire individuals and communities alike with undeviating tenacity and obedience to high moral standards in all aspects of life. The conception of the right of every individual to live his life in security and freedom from debasing influences linked with the responsibilities and vital interests of the community helped to engender a purposeful life, a life inspired and informed by the eternal spirit and glowing wisdom of the Halachah.

CLOSE

It will now be plain to the reader why I have chosen "The Humanity of Jewish Law" as the title of my book. In the preceding chapters I have tried to set down, without claim to completeness, attitudes and doctrines of an age-old and unique legal system. Circumstances and environment have diminished neither its extraordinary force nor its timeless relevance. The resolute acceptance of the Halachah by the Jewish people as its compelling guide has helped to enhance the identity and deepen the conscience of its loyal adherents.

Embracing all aspects of life and behaviour the Halachah is the authentic expression of religious and moral values. Its authority is the authority of God, Who has revealed His will through the Torah, the Hebrew Prophets and the Sages. It is Divine law designed for the welfare, spiritual and social, of the individual, the community and the nation.

The purpose of the commandments is to purify and refine the Jew. The aim of all the precepts, says Maimonides, ritual, ceremonial and ethical, aim directly and indirectly at the good life, the life of kindness, benevolence and brotherhood. The Halachah insists on the sanctity of both the written and the spoken word. The rights of the individual as well as those of the community are clearly defined and must be zealously observed. Laws and regulations govern all human relations, the family and the market place.

Special solicitude for orphans and widows is strongly urged. In their loneliness they must be shown sympathy and understanding. Lack of regard for their feelings may cause them to suffer loss of independence and self-confidence. The poor must be treated with complete impartiality. To show them favour in law would detract from their dignity and self-respect.

The Hebrew word צדקה, charity, also connotes "justice". Charity in Judaism is a legal and moral obligation as well as a corporate responsibility. The ideal charity is that which reduces hardship, alleviates distress and shows consideration for the recipient.

While the virtue of compassion is of the very essence of Judaism it did not affect the law and the decisions of the courts. Indeed, though responsive to human problems and dilemmas, the law was the supreme authority and those who administered it were not to succumb to sentimentality or emotional weakness. Their judgments were to be dominated by the judicial concepts and canons of the Halachah. Yet the Sages believed that there is a greater kind of justice dispensed by a Higher Court, more powerful and more luminous than the human courts. That Court did not always press justice to its limits. Its justice was tempered with mercy. Man owed obedience to the authority and jurisdiction of both courts.

But for its wisdom and insights, the Halachah, in the view of the Sages, would not have endured. They expressed the thought in a telling utterance preserved in the Jerusalem Talmud. "If the law had been given in the form of definitive decisions, leaving no room for differences of opinion and interpretation, it could not have survived."[1] This bold statement reflects the profundity and perception of the Jewish jurists. They applied, with impeccable zeal and judicial skill, and with reserved leniency, the principles and precedents codified in the Mishnah, debated in the Talmud, presented in the Codes and argued in the Responsa, to the problems of life in varying situations. They found support for a sound and tolerant approach in the teaching of Proverbs: "Her ways are ways of pleasantness and all her paths are peace".[2]

For the Jewish people the Halachah has been a light and inspiration amid the changing conditions under which they have lived. It has manifested a remarkable vitality and relevance.

Our generation can find satisfaction in the unusual increase and growth of Yeshivoth, Kollelim and Institutes for advanced rabbinic studies, in Israel and in other countries; the appearance of many rabbinic works and authoritative Responsa and the continuing publication of the Talmudic Encyclopaedia. They are all a measure of the renewed and keen interest in the Halachah. It is agreeable to know that there is also evidence of important research in modern Jewish legal scholarship.

And as I write the closing lines of this work a comforting thought persists in the mind even as a fervent prayer lingers in the heart: that the wide-ranging and significant contribution to Jewish jurisprudence will help to evaluate the true and deeper meaning of the Halachah which, first promulgated on Sinai — the Mountain of the

1. J. Sanhedrin 4,2
2. Proverbs 3,17

Revelation — will in future serve as the foundation of Israel's legal structure. That Israel may always carry, and proudly, our heritage and make that heritage live, religiously and spiritually, is the cherished aspiration of all those who are devoted to its welfare and its highest ideals.

In this study I have surveyed a wide field, a field well worth cultivating. Readers, it is hoped, will traverse this field more thoroughly as their tastes and ambitions prompt. They will find that the Halachah is of the head and intellect as well as of the heart and soul. To an age that has witnessed the unparalleled crimes perpetrated against fellowmen and the violent challenges to the traditional values, the humanity of the Halachah carries a warning and solemn message.

In ancient days the Psalmist saw the law as a "lamp unto my feet and a light unto my path".[3] Throughout its long and momentous history this law has illumined the thorny path of the Jewish people. Today, the House of Israel and the world stand in need of its light, its vision and its inspiration.

3. Psalm 119,105

INDEX